Puro Purismo

By

A. Razor

PUNK ★ HOSTAGE ★ PRESS

Puro Purismo
Copyright © 2021 by A. Razor
An imprint of Punk Hostage Press
ISBN **978-1-940213-10-1**

Editor
Iris Berry

Introduction
Dayna Rodela

Cover Art
Big Ray

Cover Layout
Michele McDannold

Punk Hostage Press
Hollywood, USA
punkhostagepress.com

*To my children
and their mothers.
And to my mother
may she rest in peace.*

Editor's Acknowledgements

My friendship with A. Razor began in 2006 after our mutual friend, Bucky Sinister suggested we meet. It was at Canter's on Fairfax. But we really met a long time before that in 1982, we just didn't know it. Believe it or not, it was at the US Festival, backstage in the V.I.P. section for Van Halen. David Lee Roth was my boss, I worked at his after-hours place in Hollywood, the Zero Zero Club.

It was as backstage areas go, a huge buffet with everything under the sun, and tables and chairs as far as the eyes could see, and they were all empty. All of Van Halen's guests were inside hanging with the band. It was just me and the D.J., I loved it. We had the whole place to ourselves, and I kept asking him to play Prince's, "Little Red Corvette" over and over and over. I'm gonna say he probably played it about 20 times. I'll never forget it. One day as I was telling Razor this story he said to me, "That was you?" Yes, Razor was my D.J.

Our paths crossed many times after that... We both frequented Red Stodolsky's Baroque Books off of Hollywood Boulevard, probably always just missing each other. And we hung out at the same bars and the same clubs in Hollywood. I lived at Disgraceland, and he lived down the street from me at another famous Hollywood crash pad called "Hotel Hell" at the Garden Courts Apartments.

Neither one of us knew then that we were living and participating in an important time in history, in the heart of a vital era of music and art that would change modern culture. And that the places we were living in would one day be legendary. Or that one day together we would build from the ground up a publishing company that we loved that would bring together a powerful literary community with the very D.I.Y. skills we honed in the 1980s.

A. Razor and I launched Punk Hostage Press on Friday the 13th of January in 2012, with the sole intention of publishing two books. Mine and his, *The Daughters of Bastards,* and *Better Than a Gun in a Knife Fight.* And here we are nine years later with 40 books and counting.

Some stories write themselves, ours is one of them...

In A. Razor's own words, he would like to thank, Dayna Lopez, Marc Lopez, Felix A. Montague, Ashley Montague, Monika Myers, Eva Wonder Mae Riot, Gina Gerace, Geoff Melville, Christopher Deinstag, Presh Apostoli, Becca Ivy, Ugo Machaca, David Maldonado, Kobie Grimes, Cindy Saner, Seth Kline, Gabe & Chevaun Lowry, Dave Polo, Ali Rush, Che Jordan, Jerm, Cyrus Amini, Dorian DotCom Washington, Viva Liles-Wilkin, William Sanchez, CES ONE, Teddy Quinn, Deborah Tobin, Sonny, Kevin Bone, Laura Sibley, James Sibley, James Jones, Nicci Carrante, Adolfo Communale, Joker, Deana Jean Privott, Dean Privott, Maggie Radcliffe, Scott & Yung Ota, Viva Padilla, Steve Abee, Milo Martin, Pam Ward, MK Chavez, Cassandra Dallett, Paul Corman-Roberts, Chiwan, Choi, Todd Anderson, Mark Savage, Mike The Poet Sonksen, Ellyn Maybe, Keith Martin, Jon Hess, Lindsey Wonderdome, Chupa Kristin, Universe Walker, Nicholas, Sequoia & Sienna Sanchez, Emmanuel Skinner lll, Vanessa Castro, Lee Leibrock, Jim Siegel, Jessie Keilt, Joanna Cedar, Harper Nolan, Kim Wagner, Lisa Marie Jensen, Fred Rucker, Mj Taylor, Jack Varnell, Cassandra Dallett, M. E. Rolle, Doug Knott, Adam Garrett-Clark, Jazzy Janet, Carl Rice, Nzingha Shakur-Ali, boona Cheema. Rick Lupert, Daniel Yaryan, Maw Shein Win.

And last but certainly not least, on behalf of Punk Hostage Press we'd like to express our deep gratitude for the endless support and inspiration all along the way. To those who are no longer with us; Red Stodolsky, Scott Wannberg, Mike Taylor, Wanda Coleman, Frank T. Rios, Ruth Weiss, Al Young, Danny Baker, Yvonne de la Vega, and Lee McGrevin, may they rest in peace. To all the writers at Punk Hostage Press, and to all the readers. To Luis J. Rodriguez, S.A. Griffin, Michele McDannold, Bucky Sinister, Richard Modiano, Susan Hayden. Tia Chucha, Beyond Baroque, Baroque Books, Stories Books, The Beast Crawl, The Ruskin Group Theatre, La Luz de Jesus Gallery, Canter's, Victor's, Dodger Stadium, The L.A. River, and the Hollywood Sign.

Iris Berry
Los Angeles
December 24th 2020

Introduction

A. Razor has experienced a second birth and an allowance of past and present works to converge on the same path. Where there was once deep loss and longing there is healing and forgiveness. Razor gives us silhouettes of words dancing under dim street lights and first-hand experiences in the grips of self-destruction. He shows us the beauty there is after the vultures circle, the words that remain in the sand still held us to this earth.

There is a time where the poet calls out into the emptiness of the night and what reverberates back are the words to fill the spaces within him. The poetry keeps us alive for far longer than we expected. Living only to fill the page in hopes that others will find us. There we can live forever in the solitude of our choosing. I know of a wandering man, a vagabond seeking his tribe and relentlessly trying to piece together what was lost in the fire. He searched for me for over 30 years and when I found him I found myself. The stranger in the mirror was a familiar face, the same eyes staring back at me. In his books, I found my first birthday card, candid shots from the life of a man I sought to know. Each piece a self-portrait locked in time and a map back home to oneself. The greatest gift, the words "for my lost daughter, may we meet again someday". If words kept him alive until the day we could meet again, then I will worship these words and the light they created for me to finally find my way to you.

~ *Your lost daughter*

Contents

I welcome this heavy shroud.
I want to be buried in it--
to be sculptured marble
in craftier hands.

~ Luis J Rodriguez

Apache

they were notable in how they revered the water
the precious cooling water that flowed from the
stony hillsides and mountain ravines in what is
now called new mexico and over into the land
that is now called mexico
they knew no border of nation
only tribal boundary laid down
by war and honor of battle
by footpath through mountain pass
by thunderous visions up in
the roiled skies above
by murder for survival
they were pure in their purpose
to protect the sacred water that
flowed from the springs with all
they had to call on in their human form
that the spirits of the world had given them
as vessels to reckon with through time until
they had given all they had to give at last
in the fulfillment of their born purpose
to protect the holy water from the
ravages of the land of man
the lust and greed of man
they knew it would be
coming upon them
upon the springs
upon the water
they were sworn to die
to protect it
it was what was most important
it was what gave them life
it was what gave life meaning
and so they lived
and so they killed
and so they died

Burning Saints

my grand father did this, I know
my father did this too, I was told

they burned saints, cards with saints
in effigy and prayers like poems
printed on the back

it was a ritual that came from their
homeland that was meant to show
no allegiance or moral would
interfere with the work
at hand
with the expectation
of loyalty above all
to the principle
of this thing
that was
supposedly
theirs
and theirs alone

the truth came out
eventually
it was not enough
of a gesture
to hold the rest of the world
at bay

they met their deaths
the same way they
had caused the deaths
of others
violent and fast

the ashes of burnt sainthood

have been dissolved in my blood
since before I was born
into the bastard sin of this life
I have eaten all the small fires
of card stock prayers and saints
inside my imprisoned dreams
they have made me stronger
when I was at my weakest
but, god seemed to tire
of all the empty gestures

the tally of human sin does not seem
to be of interest to god
in any cause and effect determination
that I have ever witnessed

I have traveled near and far
meeting many people
in many other places
with many other ideas
about who god is
for themselves
I put them all together
in my mind's eye
and I see the god

I see god for who
god really is

god is tired

god's eyelids droop
as god waves a
tired hand

absolving sin from the wretched demons
that have made god weary with playfulness

while we wept on river banks
wringing our hands
shaking our heads
begging for tearful forgiveness
when all we had to do
was scream loud enough
for god to hear
thy will be done

then get about
the doing
of it
right away

Genetics From My Unknown Father

his story appeared in the bloodstream at birth
he was raised on green bottles of mineral water
olive oil and fresh bread that should have made
life softer like lovers under tangled sheets on a
warm spring night that blows a hopeful wind in
through a window that opens on a moonlit view
of a shimmering Mediterranean below the cliffs
of an island outpost that was overrun by many
invaders over time so that stone hearts and icy
stares had become a birthright that never made
life in transition easy for anyone who looked back
with curious eyes of water balled into heart shaped
fantasies about what the ghost image shifting into
black shadows like something codified by other mythos
of what a figure might look like when a mantle would be
passed down onto the shoulders of what should have
been something, but never was, leaving an untellable
tale of what the missing face of a father faintly resembled
when no father was ever there in the light that came in
through the morning window that lit up the horror inside
a lonely child bent on the path that was so familiar and yet
so foreign to all the baseball cards and bubble gum that hid
the switchblades and petty thievery chained to a murderous
desire
that always whispered hoarsely inside the mind *"someone has to*
pay for what happened...someone has to pay in blood"...
even if it takes forever and forever more

Mom Remembers Little About Roswell

she is captured by her little girl desires
taken away by dreams of specialness
discovering a new world in the light
of a falling star that was her spaceship

she shows them where the light bent down
on the horizon of her little girl twilight sky

she shows them where it crashed into the ground
the smoldering wreckage drawing them closer

she is told to never speak of this vision aloud
she is told that she did not see anything at all
she is just a little girl who sees lights in the sky
as they move around her
most of the time alone

the lights talk to her like no one else does
the lights make her feel better than the dark
the dark only tells her loneliness like a little girl
should never know but many know it anyway

she flies away with the lights in her dreams
she is covered in the warmth of lights
that crash down from the sky at night
falling into velvet metal pieces
that she bends down to touch
gently at her feet
she swears to them
she will never tell anyone

a woman remembers herself
humbled by lights from the sky
crashing to the earth at her feet
being told to never speak of it
she holds her children close at night

she tells them not to fear the light
far away up in the sky as it moves
it is her secret friend of specialness
made into something else by change
something she kept quiet about
something she never forgot

the years that went by with a secret inside
she doesn't want to talk about them too much
but when she does her eyes light up bright
she lets a little secret out about specialness
it takes her away to the time of little girls
looking into the night sky for something
that might take them away from there
that might save them from a terrible
form of loneliness

she tells the secret
only a little
at a time now
little by little
she seems afraid that
if she told it all at once
she might lose that last
memory of light
crashing to the feet
of a little girl
giving her the gift
of specialness
giving her the curse
of a top secret
to keep forever
even after
the little girl
has been gone
for so long

On Duty

it is all part of the job on the night watch
the split second decisions after long interludes
of a numbing silence broken by the random
jingling of the keys on the belt

souls dying behind doors under medication
wounds that have gone unlicked so long
they have festered beyond healing
only hopes are tied to surgical
cleansing of spirits under
the fire of a broken
sanity held on to
by the last tendrils
of hollowed out love
living behind eyes of desperation

torment is the song that is sung out loud
against the internal prognosis of mistrust
against the internal experience of desert
against the reckless wreckage of abandonment
it's refrain is loudest when it is sung quietly
in the fractured minds that see hope as elusive
in its ever rapidly shifting shapes of change

on the night watch it is all about the keys
they dangle and you can curse the unholy
sound as they will themselves to combination
setting against each other like thieves in seclusion
you grasp them firmly and close your eyes to stop
the noise of metallic discordia
the silence is all you have in these moments
before the terror of upheaval nears again
rearing its ugly visage like an
ominous specter of threat
on the watch, forever on the watch

over 100 years ago...

...a huge earthquake hit the bay area and the city of san francisco burned and the gold/silver rush era ended and the bank of america was born...frisco was rebuilt and if you look at the history that has passed since then you get a view of human culture advancing in a rapid convulsion like it never has before...

everything is so much faster and bigger and overwhelming now in comparison to then...there are more people and the distance between them is lessened by technology...there is no going back, or at least that is how it seems, but the most prized thing in the human existence is still intimacy and love...

material captures the attention with spectacle, but anyone with any material can be lonely, while even the most desperately poor and downtrodden can at least find momentary shelter in intimacy and love...you can't bottle it and sell it...you can sell the illusion of it and attempt to make it permanent through ritual(marriage), but you can't make it so because it is fleeting and rare and takes so much out of a person to achieve it with another person and then it taxes while it fortifies those who share it...it is the most complex and difficult to achieve aspect of the human condition and the hardest to maintain...

i have been blessed with its presence many times in my life and paid for it in agonizing moments of pain, fear and loneliness...it can't be taken for granted, as it will never obey all the rules all the time...the best i have been able to do is appreciate it for the moment and hope the moment lasts forever...it hasn't yet...

you would think our modern world would have more of it due to our abilities to move and communicate faster, but those same occurrences are also factors in muting its presence as well...love and intimacy...

i fantasize about capturing it and holding it prisoner sometimes, my precious lil' detainee that i will never give up for security reasons, probably out of frustration that i am lacking it in profound moments that i have...or may have...

like the city ablaze all around us and the buildings falling down into piles of burning rubble...

9

deep end

thrown in for kicks
or jumped in for fun
it doesn't matter
now its time
swim or swallow
keep the head
above the surface
kick for all its worth
paddle like crazy
do whatever it takes
to keep from sinking
do it quickly
or sink
swim or swallow
keep the head
above the surface
the bottom is far below
the safety of dry land
does not seem safe enough
to move toward it just yet
this might be what it is all about
this might be what is called for
whether you were thrown in
or if you actually jumped
it doesn't matter
swim or swallow
keep the head
above the surface
if you ever want to make it
out of the deep end again

A 9 Year-Old Boy After a Funeral

it was a wrapped up legacy
hidden in the nightstand
at the bottom of the
drawer

it was handed over to the boy
in an old cigar box full
 of random mementos
 of what a
grandpa was

it was magnificent for a young boy
to behold in the moment
where he felt
a great loss that he
could not process
a grief that he
could not manage
a pain he had to keep inside
it was how it was in those days

unsheathed from the cloth that held it tight
the pearl handle so iridescently bright
the image of the boy seemed to age
in the sharp reflection of the blade
distorted as it was when it moved
ever so slightly back and forth

he is startled by the brief appearance
in the blade's shifting reflection
the light forming familiar shapes
like the ghostly face of his
grandpa behind him

the boy jerks back

in sadness and fear
he cuts his thumb open deep
the trail of blood runs quickly out
comes down across the blade
drips into a small pool
upon the dirty carpet
next to his feet

the boy shaken and in shock
his heart stills a bit
as his mind finds its bearings

this is not the end
this is just the beginning

the blood pool is growing
as the pain does too
with a throbbing sensation
that is almost hypnotic
it captures his mind
in a way he will never
forget

someday this moment
would be all he needed
to remember
when he would be
seeking to find
something
in a name
for himself

when he had lost
all hope of knowing
who he was, alone

Color Wheel

angelic white
tans beige
bleeds red
makes green
wears black
talks brown
gets pink
bruises purple
cries aqua-
marine
hides yellow
behind
blue eyed
devil

Bombs

when I was a youngster
I liked to burn things
with gasoline
I melted my plastic infantry
on their backyard battleground
I melted all my G.I. Joes
I melted all my lil' sister's
Barbie dolls and even
her Barbie penthouse
went up in molotov flames
I learned to mix the perfect
molotov
taught by errant biker's
Nam vets and assorted
gangsters that were very
helpful to young pyros
growing up in the Berdoo heat

in a coke bottle
half filled with gas
a quarter used motor oil
a quarter palmolive
wax on top
m-100 duct taped
to the side
a great incendiary performance
inside abandoned buildings
in a desert city that was always ready
to spontaneously combust

I caught the eye of a man with a dark past
who saw I had knack for the bomb
he taught me about timed charges
the nobel history of dynamite
the compact ingenuity of C-4

how car ignitions were great
machines of bombastic destruction
the last thing his victims knew
were the sickening realization
that the car was not starting properly
he had grown up in Detroit
during world war 2
he had played with the fire like I was doing
he had learned the skills he was passing to me
from another man with a darkened past
working for gangsters that wanted to eliminate
each other, then one day he had to eliminate the man
who had taught him the trade
now he lived in anonymity
at the thunderbird motel on mt. vernon blvd.
drank scotch and sodas at the san-hi lanes bowling alley
in the darkened bar, quietly biding his time
his explosive past a lonely secret
that he shared with a young boy
along with the knowledge of vengeful death
underneath the carriage of an automobile
waiting for the key to turn a lifetime into oblivion

the day I went to see him for advice on how
to make a shaped charge I was going to use
to dismantle the hulk of a stolen car abandoned
in the desert wash below Devore
I found the room vacant at the thunderbird
the maid saying he had been found dead that morning
she had seen me come around a lot in the last year
on my schwinn stingray or my hobie skateboard
she asked me, very politely
if I knew who his family was
I told her he was my uncle
but that no one else in the family
spoke to him anymore
she gave me his bag of tools

and a box with old clocks and watches in it
and when I blew up the abandoned car in the wash
the very next day
I figured it was better this way
I didn't think I would have been up to
blowing him up
as my first victim

Government Cheese

she lived on the wrong side of the tracks
and was always crossing over
one way or the other
she hated the smell of her life
and the taste of lies
and the sound of confessions
and the way it all looked
over her shoulder
as she crossed the tracks
going away from it
and especially
looking straight at it
on her way back home
usually early in the morning
when no one would notice
her coming and going
until one day it caught up
with her
and she choked to death
on a moldy toast
and government
cheese sandwich
and she made it
to the tracks
before collapsing dead
not quite on any
side, but more
in the middle
of it all

Puro Purismo

clashing cultures underneath sun gods and smog
heaving piles of humanity into chaotic lines
of boulevard demarcation
of avenue border separation
of street life possibilities
on the back road of identity
in crisis, in stasis, in terrified moments
of self-loathing catastrophes
coming undone at the edges
when you feel no acceptance
anywhere you go in this battlefield
that has been strategically filled in
with landmines that hide
just beneath the surface
of a land covered in skin
that tans dark under the
summer sun
but, can turn pale enough
in the wintertime
matched with blue eyes
for the cold front
so pale, in fact
that someone you love
says you are passing
for your enemy
these words that you feel
all underneath the skin
that constantly betrays you
as a person who belongs
to no one, really
your identity becomes
purely expendable
to the world at large
your sadness for this life
is purely your own
as pure as the alien snow

falling like a miracle
in the distant Mojave
coating the cracked brown origin
of the driest lake bed
with an icy whiteness
that melts away
under the purest rays of sunlight
smashing down on this barren landscape
of lost ghosts made up of the purity in their souls
this is all anyone will ever leave behind underneath this sun
this will be the only thing that is pure forever
even in the winters that last a lifetime

Suicidal Tendencies '77

most thieves never want to get caught
most thieves never do
unless they want to
get caught
to be found out
or if they know
they can steal like this forever

it all seemed like thievery to the boy
who saw it all in daydreams as he
became slow to do chores for an
allowance that would become
working wages that he saw
was a death sentence to
everyone as mysterious
men in suits and ties
were lauded for their
intelligence as they
took all the profit
from the dying
labor of others

the boy didn't see it as politics and didn't want
any part of it, just seemed like fancy thievery
to his inexperienced eyes

at 15 he had an epiphany, brought on by
a large dose of malt liquor, weed and angledust
after an epic surfing session
amidst the wreckage
of Pacific Ocean Park Pier
he would follow the way he had been warned to avoid
he knew the odds by then, figured if he made it to 25
he'd have beaten them all
so he made a suicide pact

with his closest friends
nothing after 25
to stop the thieves
that were already here
before he had ever
been born

A Simple Pause

don't throw out bathwater
even when babies are not present
because the real love is always held together
in the dirt that sinks to the bottom of the basin
in the raw flesh exposed from a good washing
the tenderness of everything kept in order by chaos
if you hesitate you save the possibility, but always keep it
moving
even when you pause a moment over bathwater decisions
because there will always be a light at the end of every tunnel
until the light is omnipresent, even inside the longest tunnels
or the ceiling collapses before you make it out alive
at which point the moment you took to consider a rash action
might have saved something better than being trapped alone
in a tunnel with rash decisions and damaged impulses
slowing breathing in the last breath of conscious choice
without a baby left to cry for you
or even a splash of bathwater comfort
in the slowly enveloping darkness

Bury My Heart At Chavez Ravine

the world encroaches
a little more each day
the songs of the chumash
and the children of slavery
that lined the steep walls
in a lean to existence
as the rain rolls down the sides
and the wind blows in the
other direction
the memories get scattered
and washed out with the blood
along a concrete lined river bottom
and the water runs underground
under the shame of the hottest
rays of sunlight
and the people clamor
for azure draped heroes
above the din
of the sacred spirits
as they wail and moan
for justice and peace
and a new home
or at least an empty space
that would be a hollow monument
in the mega mall ideas
that collect like dry leaves
on the planning boards easel
as they push for development
over the parched bones that
belonged to the Takic words
that were ground into dust
and became the chalk outline
of a diamond
on a field of play
and amid the cheers
for every home run

is a scream of horror
and pain
that echoes across
the tops of the
trees near the dog
trodden paths
that outline the futile
escape routes
of an ancient
migration
away from progress
and into a peaceful
moment
after the troops cleared
the last of the
shelter
and the plans
began
for the
ball park
because the grass
is always money green
in the centerfield
of dodgertown

Hanging on a Star

come run away with me
come see the world with me
come into this womb
come into this moment
into this belief of love

she wants to believe in him
like she believes songs on the radio
might be about her indirectly
but, of course, she knows
it is not really about her

there is no reason behind it
no reason is necessary for it
no reason to believe in it
no facts to support it
come here now anyway

take the greatest chance ever

come make a wish come true

jump into unknown love with abandon
leave your dreams in a pile on the floor
where you can see them in the moonlight
that pierces in through the little window

wish on a star wish on a rainbow wish on a wishbone
close your eyes so tight and wish so hard you see stars
then when the stars go away and you can see clearly again
leave through the door you believed to be your gateway
into a world you called home and a life you called love

Lineage

these words drip out of minds
        out of hearts
             out of mouths
        off of fingertips
tributaries of life leading toward rivers
        spilling out into vast oceans
        of poems spoken over
          time
        into the air breathed in
        into the hearts on fire
        into the unknown

these poets are born with poetics internalized
                words as imaginary playmates
        arranging themselves in a child's mind
          ideas in opposition become
        contrast for layered images that form hope
          children weep alone
        with words as their only salvation
          no one knows why
        they cry the tears of poets
          they grow trees with tears
          forests with time

these years go by until middle aged people become poetic
          blood having been saved enough
        words bleed out into designs that are natural
          filling the lines of movement full
        collecting names for tombstones forgotten
          announcing names of births yet to be
        a cadence becomes a rhythm of language
          a child's hope is tempered in fires
          burned of regrets
          the hottest flame
          leaves this faith

a poet toils with a thousand names past
>*a poet dies trying to write a thousand more*
>>a sign of nobility in cowards
>always brings down a vengeful scream
>>a sign of fear in lovers
>always brings down an anxious moment
>>only the tears of children
>feed these forests we have forsaken
>>only the blood of poets
>can wash away our common disease
>>this is how we know what is really

free
>*we are just the living in the*

beginning

>>*after that we are no more*
>>*we are just the cup of redemption*
>>*offered for the sacred truth*
>>>*speak it carefully with measure*
>>>*let your tongue slip hot*
>>>>*before the cold takes it all*

these are just words
this is just another poems of sorts
put here in my head when I was just a child
remembered here by the dying embers of my life
sent back to you through my heart as it feared it was lost
spoken with my mouth through the fingers that make the words
these are just words
>*magnificent in their ancient beauty*
wholesome in their final peace
>may you always read them well
even when your heart destroys mine

Heathen

I am on the run tonight
from the memories of
past judgment and
failed futures
I cut the lines that
run down the middle
of the road
with wild swerving
maneuvers that are
barely cloaked in
the luminescent
darkness that
shrouds the industrial
part of town
I feel a pervasive
sense of life's coil
unwinding
as the road
rolls by in torrents
of blackness lashed with
iridescent lines that promote
some order to my direction
I am tempted to lose control and
drive into walls and objects
but the feelings pass almost as
fast as the lights and the painted stripes
that seem to demarcate my life from my end
and as all that life and feeling and light and
world trail past me
I feel like I might have lost what was
in pursuit of me and
what I had been in pursuit of
all at once
and I was left to wonder
which I would miss more
and which I would need less

as if the whole thing could be
divided that easily
into separate sides
of reality
when you are
traveling
at this
speed

A Song I Remembered from 1979

when wanda coleman sang that night
every atom in my heart did a do si do
turning it's partners round and round
my heart would never be the same again

when wanda coleman sang that night
the music was the truth in every word
the way she gave it all out in every breath
the way breathing would never be the same again

when wanda colemn sang that night
I found a new form of courage
that did not require smoke or drink
as it eased my lonely heart that was
barely surviving a missing adolescence

when wanda coleman sang that night
I forgot about my girlfriend turning tricks
all night long on hollywood blvd. alone
I forgot about how far away I felt from hope
with no idea where I would sleep that night
I missed home and wanted to travel far away
all in the same precious moment of breath
I learned more about fear and love as she spoke
her honest beam of song words into my heart
than I had learned from any source of knowledge
from before that night or any source of knowledge
ever since

when wanda coleman sang that night
I heard the song in the words of her poems
the singing has never stopped
the music has never stopped
it is a song that sings loudest
when I take my most labored breath

as I sing along with the song that comes in words
never to forget the song I heard that night
when wanda coleman sang that night

Ciudad de Los Angeles

they speak of angels often in the place where I was raised
everything was named as if it were a holy attachment
connected to an angry god that sent his forsaken
battered children into a desert wilderness
next to an oily seashore of lost teardrops
that was the summer playground of the
wealthiest kings who laughed in their
drunken debauch of every sacred
name ever given to the home
of the unforgiven meek
who lost every inch
to the greediest
one percent
as they bought
it all up
for nothing
only to rent
it all away
for
everything
the angels
had left
for them
forever &
forever more

It Howls and It Hums

these days the typers are glowing
and interconnected to each other
the words have eyes and find their
own way most of the time
like that character played by an
older bogart in the barefoot contessa
feeling the sound of never again being the
center of the world, the eye of the storm
long passed and even its edges have left a
dullness to the elements of climate and control
and we weave in and out of various states of disrepair
like the leftovers of the studio system walking around
hollywood in 77, ready to tell you what it was like and
to drop names that were dead or dying in rest homes
near tarzana, the last concessions were made and the
agreement was film would go to school and learn a more
predictable formula that they may convert celluloid to ticker
tape
to digital read out that swims by on the shiny new digital
billboards
proclaiming "see how cost effective and efficient we are?" as if
disney
and warner and mayer and thalberg would have ever made it
that way
there is a reason why black and white doesn't sell anymore
there is a lack of compassion toward passion
there have been roses laid on graves since before edison sent
the
pinkerton's to burn the rabble that brought his camera out west
valentino is in a cemetary that shows talkies on saturday night
he rolls in his crypt and is less remembered each day
smugness seems to always win the fight and even welles
greatest film
was re-cut years after he died and still goes unnoticed by most
you can't make them pay because they only run on credit
anyway

the little hard driven people who cut and paste away the world with
mouses and clicks and fear that they killed it accidentally thinking it was
already dead before they came upon it
this dust on the wind was once flesh and bones of those
who never made it into the credits or the by lines
never had a chance to keep a flame burning
in a world that moved so fast as that

Partisan

can't go much further
can't take much more
can't see too clearly
in the early morning
before dawn

waiting like a newly formed bud
at the end of a fragile stem
tight as a dying fist
pushing flower petals
into its tiny belly

waiting like an aging bullet
a chambered round in a
darkened pistol
facing a barrel
full of dusty
grooves

everything loose has fallen away
after the last shakedown
all things inside have tightened
into balled up desperation

silent into the night
silent into the night

feet don't make a sound
teeth don't chatter
when clenched so tight
breath is slow and shallow
wheezing when it is allowed

nothing is smoked up
nothing is drunk down
no chances are taken

be still
be still

wait
then
strike
like
it is
your
only
hope

your
last
hope

now
and
for
ever
more

Awash

nothing can save these words
scattered across the virtual 7 seas
like shipwrecked victims
after poseidon claims
what was his all along
this format is his
pointed trident
plunged upward
from the depths
into the heart
of verse once
free
now
encumbered
by technical
tragedy
like waves
washed against
the clay tablets
that held the first
poems of true love
now dissolved
for all time
becoming
salted
crust
on
dying
lips

Books I've Read and Discarded

I am a voracious
reader and seldom
take the time to
pause to ascertain
the damage
I have done

to the books

themselves

their spines broken
on the first anxious
parting of their pages
that get worn, torn
dog-eared
ripped out

their jackets
warped by
the elements

spilled drinks

burnt spoons

blackened pipes

smoldering ashes

splattered blood

errant bodily fluids

bottles and glasses

that leave circular stains
that appear like demonic halos
haunting the covers forever

I have pawned them off
in desperate moments
for petty cash to
greasy fingered
collectors
so I could get
well again
for a brief
moment

I have left them all behind
because I have had to
travel so light
move so fast
fly so high
swim so far

books can get
so heavy
so cumbersome
as I crawl on my belly
or jump from a window
or run across the
border at night

but, I would never
use a book I loved
to block a bullet
or a blade

I look in the past
at all the titles
that I mistreated
that I have lost

in this way

at the incidental
wear and tear I have done
to the source of my knowledge
that shaped all of the experiences
I have ever known
that were acquired with the aid of
their mistreated pages

the source of my inspiration
for life and creation
that emanated from the
display of words ordered
like arranged flowers
of sacred ink

I humbly offer up my service in
mending any books that I can
as I read them more gently than
ever before
placing them back
on shelves
walking away slowly
in case I might
hear them

choking
back tears
as I leave

Last Mission Before The Armistice

the bombers never left our sides
with their sights set on cities
wallowing in the earthy
plains below us

they loaded up on explosive issue
that was poured forth from above
out of gaping belly bomb bay doors
spilling out death from on high
dropping all pretense of peaceful purpose
letting the target have it all in ordinance

prayers rise up on smoke curled clouds
whole forsaken worlds call upon fate
to deliver a payload of mercy
in the twisted aftermath
the burning wreckage
the seething cauldron
the hopeless shelter
of life balanced in the cross hairs
that lie below the priority targets
sitting in the stillness
of dust and ash settled
on the lifeless ruins
of what we once were
maybe what we could have been
had triumph not been so dear to us all in the end

Potlatch

give and let give
give into it all
give until it
hurts
it feels good
to give
so much

give unto us, o lord

thankful for the giving on this one day every year
to signify the start of winter shopping sprees
push the limits of commerce to save us all
the rich are about to get even richer
so don't forget to give
even if you gave
at the office

beware the day of the natives come bearing the keys and deeds
to their casinos and reservations
as they say
"here you are, we have built these up as much as we possibly
could
and now we return your noble generosity."

the gift of giving might be given back in return
the gift of living might have been an illusion
all along

these buffalo did not return for you
as you cry inside empty casinos
from a lonely fear

suddenly, the electricity is gone from the world

how many of you speak in the rhythm of drums?
how many of you know what the smoke signals mean?

it is a gift that keeps giving
as your dugout canoe
takes on more water
than your tin cup
can bail out
efficiently

Trial Offer

the killer spoke in vowels
the jury spoke in consonants
together they would play the
most drawn out game of
hangman ever meant
to be played as a
rule of law with
no verdict
necessary
to dangle
feet just
above the
ground as
gravity did
the work of
moral syllables

Backpack Dealer

I ride on a bicycle
& I live
in a little hole
& I have my
backpack on
come on, baby
let's have some fun
you are just a little girl
mixed up in a crazy world
& when that world
comes all undone
you'll wanna have some fun
so come with me
cuz fast I can run
you'll keep up
if you really
want someone
& if you really
want to have
some fun
& if you really
want to know
I ride on a bicycle
& I live
in a little hole
and I have my
backpack on
so, come on, baby
let's get this done
I got a razor
but I won't
cut you
I keep it safely
inside my shoe
I got some gum
that we can chew

45

I got a pill for me
& a pill for you
& a pill for your friend
if she wants one, too
& then I got two
ideas about what we can do
saying I just wanna
have some fun
with you
I ride on a bicycle
& I live
in a little hole
& when I put
my backpack on
that's when you
know I'm done

Beautiful

they call this the hour of the midnight garden
she comes into it with her ideas
she comes into it with her selves
her lips dance out into smiles

light changes darkness by contrast
heart changes blood by movement
eyes see only the beauty of the world
eyes that want for more imagery

like drunks set upon a mermaid
in a poem by neruda
she is there like that
naked like truth that is never told, only felt
casting her hopes like flowers on the water
blocking out the obscenities of drunken persecution
washing her feet into fins that swim fast away

if only her hopes held enough water to carry her
across oceans to all continents that she may
bear witness to all that is beautiful

if only her faith looked upon placid waters
that sent back her reflection of her twin sister
so that both selves may know all that is beautiful

if only the golden light could stay forever on her
glimmering into her features like dancing embers
above a desert fire on a starry night to behold
all the diamonds of her heavens turning back into ash
then blown away on a wind caused by her kisses

her lips dance out into smiles across her face as it glows
with wonderment
ancient love shines off of her gaze like a beacon

guiding hearts to safe passage
as long as the captains are strong
as long as the captains are true
no harm comes to the seafaring people
as she swims alongside them
giving them the sight that they will never forget
like moments under stars shining seen from hilltops
above cities of light surrounded by
oceans of darkness
like fires burning all across landscapes stretching
beyond all seen horizons
out into space
like flowers under moonlight parading light into shadows
of changed color shades
defining delicate features
her hands shade breasts and belly
her face lined with inner light
so bright it radiates outward
her hope knows no boundaries
her dreams know no time constraint
her purpose has been incarnate forever
inward and outward
beautiful
always

Time Piece

I wanted love
I wanted to be friends
but, I couldn't shake
the image of an adversary

so I made myself
into a time bomb
and placed myself
at your front door step
and rang the bell

but, I was never
brought inside
because a time bomb
can't be trusted

so I fell apart
and all that was left
looked like a broken
wrist watch
that is kept on the dresser
just for looks

you can't tell if its real
or an imitation
it would take too much
time and effort
to tell the difference
for certain

it might be too cheap to fix
and it looks too expensive
to throw away

it has ceased to function

properly, but still
it looks good
for its
age

Devil's Ink Well

what would you do for just a taste?
sell something precious? something priceless?

what would you do after the taste was gone?
search for more? forever? for as many lifetimes as you could?

this is an endless spill even after it has ended
blotter paper with fingerings all over it
the outcome trying to be handled as much as possible
these are impossible times, these last million years
can you spot your own timeline near the ending?
this spill is a raging tide that has washed away untold empires
all of these
empires
known and unknown
have been rendered into
the screaming ghosts that drive our most industrious minds

worry not, there are no placebo gods or goddesses
or ungendered savior of indenture to this craft
you either spasm words through your mind
with uncontrollable insanity driving it along
or you fall into a silence of cocooned madness
either way your mind is driven into patterns of speech
or a dark silence that is foreboding as the questions asked
before the pen is dipped into a well that was always bottomless
with no sign of reckoning the depths no matter how sharp the
point
that has been forcibly plunged inward for every fill

sign your name on the dotted line with your own blood
as the blood of those who came before you
is already in the well
that is waiting to hear
what you might have to say about it

blowing the smoke out of windows

these statements on being
have nailed shut the
last escape route of
the damned

in youth we had fear
of magnetic fields
alien invaders
nuclear wars
godless politics
of embodied economics
...the fear left us...
replaced by shutters
that were replaced by
blinds that were
replaced by tinted
dreams of tech
without limits
connected to paydirt...

...connected to a
jackpot frenzy of...

what you would never
expect
except
it was there all along
passing us by just
to keep up with this
syntactical error
like heartbeats skipping
across golden ponds
where we were frightened
children under flags of god

...we are evolving...into...???

(what we perceive as eternal)...
it drips and it flows
...what once were ashtrays
becoming diamonds
are now diamonds
becoming paper cuts...
(these wounds are self-inflicted)

this loss is rampant
perception
turned physical
ignited then
turned to
smoke

smoke is first inhaled then
(smoke gets blown)
away
across
from afar

what once were common
hallucinations caused by
shadows in a childhood
bedtime terror are now
twenty four hour news
satellites that drop nuclear
vision through cellular osmosis
that has become what we are...
...in the face of what we are
becoming
unbecoming
as it may seem...

...transformation is the destination...

the porters all hurry to close the last
windows of opportunity because the

smoke is not just blowing out the
exit strategy any longer...
it is blowing into the mental lung
of an ironless future generation
dawning across the glowing horizon...

these are the mystical embers
that produce no heat or light

...laughter and tears pervade...
curtains went out of fashion
before they were necessary...

love became a pantomime of
lanterns without lampshades
in a digital theater of the new
adolescent pantheon made up of
mirrored windows that never open
onto three dimensional applications
with the freshest air replaced by
air freshener... with the
new smokes that have
no fires...

...evidently...
evolution does not come that easy
nor is it ever done with us

Good Morning

in the waking hours
of a winter morning
pulling on life
from the source
to get the spirit back
in your mouth, heart, lungs, mind,
eyes, limbs, ears, fingers, nostrils
fill it up to level and then
let it overflow into the
first moments of
consciousness
until it becomes awakened
with your movements
and the still born
lifelessness
is washed away
and the sensation
that is felt as a
slight tingle
and then a
warming throb
rubs against your first
thoughts of static
clarity
and you say
"Good Morning"

Suicide Girl

institutional paint on hallway walls
that lead to the door that opens into the
cold, bright room
that is full of polished, stainless steel doors
  approach the one that the man in the
  lab coat has selected and is opening, watch closely
  as the tray is slid out in front of you, look down
              at her,
              pause

  for as much time as you can,
  don't move, don't even
        twitch,
 take it all
    in,
ignore the dried blood, the burns and discolorations,
the gaping wound, the missing bone and flesh,
      the one open eye that is
       glazed over and
       looks back at you
        all lifeless,
there is nothing there,
    she had left before you had arrived
    for the last time, once again,
    and you had hoped to find
    a note or a sign that she
    would be waiting for you
    somewhere, maybe a familiar place
        you both knew
but there was nothing, so finally you break the spell
of silence, and your voice echoes through the cold, cavernous
room
stabbing you in the ears as it returns,
       "yes, i know her. that is
her."
and the man slides the tray
back into the wall and closes

the stainless steel door
and the sound of the latch catching
                      reverberates
                      in your heart
the man in the lab coat leads you
to an area with a table and some paperwork
and your mind goes blank so you can fill out
all of the forms
and you decide on cremation, fire
                      is to be her final resting place,
                            ashes to be strewn out
                         under your tears
                         as you realize
                         for the last time
                          that it is too late
                          for goodbye

    she is gone from this place forever
                      your suicide girl

Dia de Los Muertos

bones don't fade away as fast
as all the other parts do

they are easier to remember
they are simple to remember

they dress up with feathered head dress
they dance festively around the plaza

these are the bones that tell
the ancient stories of struggle
in the cities of angels that have
made their wings into decorations
for their empty celebrations
they no longer have the knowledge
of flying with their own wings freely
they have forgotten they are angelic

spirits must be guided into hearts
spirits only understand the directions
that only the bones can give them
they wander looking for the answers
losing flesh and blood along the way
spirits search for bones in everything
they lament the day that they will
find no more bones in anything

burn bonfires along the shoreline at night
light the way for all the lost spirits that are
searching blindly in the darkness by night
in the early morning the smoldering embers
give the warmth to the fallen angels that are
walking along the oceans edge by day
searching for the feathers that were once
the beautiful wings they soared with

as they left their bones behind
sailing into the freedom of the heavens
leaving lonely bones behind
leaving all these bones behind
forgetting the tales of the body
forgetting the words of the body
forgetting the art of the body
but never the names they knew
at the altar of the temple
but never the art they made
at the altar of the temple
where it will never be
forgotten
as long as it is
remembered
by you
in your heart

pray for those angels to take up their wings
pray for the true saints to be resurrected
from the sinners who fear their own bones
pray for the song of the holy temple
built on ground hallowed by winged words
worshiped by vision made real in life
worshiped by vision made real in spirit

place the names from the temple
at the altar with care
with loving beats of
hammer against nails
pounding out the
songs of laughter
in joyful
memories

the altar in the hills carries names beyond
the world of words known only to angels

the world of words known only to bones

these names travel like spirits across time
they seek the company of hearts
they seek the company of love
they find it inside of you
as you find your wings
guided by these bones
like smoke on the wind
above the smoldering ashes
of bonfires on beaches
lit long ago

these fires that give warmth
these fires that give light
these fires that give love

they burn brightly inside
bones of ash
spirits of wind
cities of angels
temples of man

How God Got Played While We Were Busy Playing God

there was light once
brighter than any sun
that is no longer seen
only spoken of as
miracles
that you have to have
faith in
or you just go mad
telling stories
of someone else
of another salvation
you never could have known
missing your own with a
a jealous craziness
somewhat akin to
government and religion

Desperation

out play the dealer
beat the odds
raise the stakes
I am sawed off at the
knees and chest like a
shotgun that can be
hidden under a dirty
trench coat and can be used as
a persuasive device against
an unwilling authority figure
to hopefully induce a little release
on the pressure that is building as
the clock ticks and the bankrupt
morality play carries on a diversionary
advertising campaign so the f.b.i. sniper
team can gain a better position on the
opposing high ground
their sweating trigger fingers
never shake
never miss
it is just
another
job...
elimination

As The Grip Finally Loosens A Bit
for Will

you are never toothless, even if you are missing all your teeth
you can still bite back, bite the wrong thing, bite the right thing
you can never use your mouth for anything better than to just
give the simplest words of support, loud as they may be
digging in like tempered spades of heavy excavation
unearthing the hidden truth as they cower a bit, shaking
trembling at the raspy harsh love loud with spittle
and curse and intention to erode the coverage of false fearful
pasts
you are always present in the bellowing throat laughter that
will
never stop echoing around the rooms of the heart or
the card tables where death is cheated by your toothless grin
holding cards so perfect like fake teeth that bring every round
home
every round you make all night pacing the floors of uncertain
outcomes
no time for bullshit or gallantry among the broken down souls
that require
focus now words now action now meaning now clear cut
convictions now
it all spills out onto worn down heels that kick back and watch
as it all
unfolds like bills on the table as you ante up for the call and
death, well,
death just smiles back at you with your own teeth and you
know for sure
he is really getting tired of being cheated by you now
your last hand was not so spectacular at all
but the bluff was always amazing until the end
as the bony hands of your nemesis scraped all the winnings to
his side of the table
you smile back at him, the last laugh is yours
blowing smoke in his face, your mouth smiles defiant
because you knew along

you never needed teeth to bite back, anyway
because
even without teeth,
that mouth made noise that will never be forgotten

Medicinal

she dances in twist & turn
rounded moves into the curves
of arching wants
she moves with the rhythm of rainfall across glass
timpani on the windowpane accompanied by crackled logs
placed carefully in the hearth of sickly desires
she holds it together, the space you are a part of
eyes darting into soulflesh like lancing a thousand heartaches
pouring out all the bitterness of the left behind, the life alone
for the moment, the blend is into one
the pour is slow syrupy goodness
it might lie about tomorrow as it lies next to love
only because it can't escape the moment
anymore than you can
with interlocking fingers
tangled up locks of hair
crisscrossed arms & legs
rocking back & forth
riding up & down
rolling round & round
writhing in & out
settling for nothing more than a cure
a medicinal allotment of precious joy
surging through the inner cosmos
doing all the lovely damage
on the inside
she takes up all she can bear
walks away from all the neglecting thoughts
takes her time in the other room
mingles with the other people
& you swear it was something that was taken away
from you before she came, now it has gone
as if she could leave with that which was never there
walking off into a distant music
to dance away from here

to dance away from you
& you say
let love lead me where it may

Moon Park Mind

crisp air changes seasons
streets here change nothing
moons beam back full amounts of light
words kiss inside minds making warm thoughts
sounds of footsteps coming down memory lane
it is all about the make out session
in the backside vinyl head rest
in the back water parking lot
of eccentric thoughts
over teapots for two
from midnight to one
in the lazy neon
that fades away
into a brisk walk
in the orb lit park
with thoughts of
self
thinking
about each other
in dreams that are
never had

As The Lady Deals Another Spade
for Mike Taylor

you told me this would happen
I will always follow your lead
the words always mean more
than people tend to realize
the words are where we worship
the words are the mountain
the words are the river
at it's holy source
the words are the beach
& the ocean that shapes it
the words are the temple
we bowed at together
you are the words
that I have read
that I have heard
for now
forever
you are the words
I will remember
always

Mohican

the first of the Mohicans was never written about
she was spoken of in round after round of words
told in an ancient language that meant people
as a part of a whole creation , as a part of a creator
an ancient language that has been nearly obliterated

she was a mother of many nations, many tribes
all people need a great mother that is loved
by a creator that gives love as creation
she was a mother of words spoken out loud
the words were spoken to be passed down
to be remembered for their meanings
every breath a drumbeat of thump on skin
every sound a teaching to draw out love
in the unborn children of a harsh survival

many years this makes the way clear, cuts a path
the land is part of creation, the parts are joined
seamless they bend in and out of each other
the stories weave with the words told by fires
the culture is not a concept, it is an action that is lived
until it meets machined blades, bullets and pox

many years this goes on as words are lost
ties to creation are interfered with by invaders
hope gets abused into smoke as fires go untended
connections are interrupted, the words are in peril
they are not words in this language, so it is not noticed
until the desire rises up to take back lost words

smoke words get confusing, hearts work fast against fate
never fast as the armies that rise up, the word culture was
never necessary before this time, the fires get stoked
the fores get extinguished, lit up again, put out
lit up again and again as fire comes into water

fire comes into metallic wonder of death machines gone mad
fire is still there to guide silent walks into wilderness nights

the burning sage, copal and tobacco summon forth new hopeful
era
the thunderbird is broken winged but returns with skyfires aloft
the coyote is a trickster that is never easy to find out, anyways
the FBI is determined to lay siege to your last word in your
mind
your last word in your heart, the last word of creation that
escapes you
the action is not exactly warrior or revolutionary as it is
reactionary
the movement stops for no one, the fires must be kept alive
this what a creator will do with its parts over time
buffalo taken away to come back as conspirators
owls left to be blinded lookouts for peaceful terms
crows with sharpened wits scramble to scavenge bits
wolves slink for cover as copters shoot from above
snakes seek cold blooded politics as they rise to fame
jackrabbits skip away into self-medicated oblivion games
the turtle is left to hide in the last lodge of refuge, it's shell
the buffalo dying out in defiance across concrete prairies bare
their broken teeth and chemo ravaged hides to the elements
as they are turned ravenous with a well-earned rage filled
psychosis
turning on each other as much as they push back against the
power of it all
the power of the uncreator that is uncreating everything it can
for the sake of it
the power that has been laying waste to the world in a corrupt
series of crusades
that have never won the day for the cross they bare up from
cavalry to claim
an immanent domain of passage and mortgage on the souls of
the words spoken around fires long before the deeds were ever
written on paper

Lay On Down Here

a bed of stones to lay down upon
to rest the remnants of burning embers
going cold as they are fading in brilliance
extinguished desires that once were flames leaping high
they fall upon the stones for a forgiving end to the light
a blinding light they once spread across the night sky
like a beacon of faith that dwindled into hope
as it faded in its brilliance and faltered slowly
only to become lost dreams with no momentum
cooling cooling cooling cooling
just wisps of smoke curling outward
laid down for the final moment before eternal sleep
the eyes like windows of a broken soul now shuttered
closing up as if the storms were upon the shores now
no more a lighthouse in the tempestuous world of stones
these rock beds hold the foundations that life was born upon
it is only fitting it should find a place upon them to be forgiven
for the unforgiving demands that their fleshy lips have made
upon the hardest part of the world that gives the softest part
a final bed from which to view the sky one last time
then it will be good night forever
as stone beds becoming blankets
become heavens below us
that finally become us

In A Park Of Echoes

scorched earth daydreams
trample sacred tongues
into mortal remains
barely standing

the sound of songs sung out loud
echoes off of the brick tenement walls
into the empty parking lot
of last goodbye times

cockroaches scurry down the boulevard
past doorways that open into lost hearts
they never saw this coming in their worst
slash and burn sexual affairs that lacked
enough cigarettes to leave lipstick on butts

the small body of water is still unequal to the amount
of teardrops that fall in a long night time of regrets
that linger in the frets like broken guitar strings
dangling happiness like baited hooks for
wild spiderfish come crawling for victims
to drag back down into the darkest part
of the shallow waters near the boathouse

statuesque beauty honors the upward spray of fountains
by standing guard on the last glimmers of neon twilight
that border the windows of the last taco truck stand off
looking out into the shadows that cast fires against the hills

the fires never go out here or lose control of their heat
the water never clears away the dust from the corners
the air never stays clean enough to breathe in at last gasp
the earth carries the burden of progress while ancient law
sways the palm trees into a motion that keeps the bats from
sleeping tonight among the fronds

over and over again
rippling
then
returning
once more

A Little Short On Insight

she wanted to see fancy tattoos
but all I had was bad scar tissue

she wanted to read my latest novel
but all I wrote was bad poetry

she wanted to see danger like I had seen,
live on the edge, conquer the fear
but all I wanted was a
safe and quiet
place to sleep it off

she wanted to love me if I
would only love myself
but I could only love her

she wanted me to be strong
and brave
but all I could show were signs
of insanity and breakdown

and when she left me behind
I just drank and used and
fought and fucked the pain away
and I laid there in the wreckage
of it all, so glorious, so wretched

and in a peaceful moment
of nothingness
I wondered how she could
have ever loved me
if she had never
been fulfilled

Aqualung

auditorium of visions
see into sounds
life in a fishbowl
too far down
burrowing into
multicolored rocks
too far up
ascending
out of water
for a moment
for too long
for nothing
no wasted motion
can be afforded
for air
for life
for nothing
that is left
just keep on
swimming around
in the in between
so there is
so there can be
flow
flowing
through and across
through and through
thoroughly
through
it all
water
breathing

apogee

pear blossom and periwinkle in lavender tones
contrast the outlines of childhood bones

wristwatch & back draft burns down the world
loneliness in ashes as flags are unfurled

honeydew and applesauce with sugar & spice
never ask to borrow another loser's vice

shrill sounding sirens wail across town
no one here left to dig in the ground

they say what goes up always comes down
so far from the surface the center's not found

superficial circumference is too far around
stand tall in the place that never was sound

letters are numbered in the words you are bound

this is where it all pulls away from us
spinning out into the vast nothing
never to return, unless   unless

Chevelle

she turns fast and tight
as we pass on a desert highway
coming close enough to
each other in the darkness
to nearly trade paint
to definitely trade fake names
as loud rock n roll blared
over whiskey talk and beer bottle
philosophies

she dances it off and avoids
any form of collision that
involves a commitment to
tongues or hearts

she dances it off in the back room
under the fluorescent black lights
barefoot, sans heels, nakedness
pressed to me like candy paint
on my old school chevelle

every layer is an aesthetic illusion
of unrequited love splashing
into the desert sand
like liquid sunshine

I breath deep for a whole song
taking in the rapturous smell
of synthesized tropical fruit

when the last song
is finished she
kisses my cheek as
she smokes her tires
escaping through the curtain
her smile still lingering in the tired

mind behind lonely, traveling eyes
still weary from the road

Finish

you can't see the fingers wiggle
through the blood on your hands
some days here

the work is never done
until you are done
with it

hold on to your dreams
until your vision is blurred
from too many tears
then hold on
some more

walk it off like a big cramp
or a broken leg
at least you can
still walk

give something back even though
you lost it all and when they call
from an 800 number just
tell them the truth
"I got nothing left
and nothing is coming"
you can add
"have a nice day"
if you are
strong enough
in the moment

take it all in like a deep breath
you paid for that privilege
in a market crisis and the
value may be less now

but there is no interest
on the coughing gasp
for more

you are still alive
despite the odds
or the predictions

you run the race
anonymous

no number
or insignia

just another
face in the
crowd
clamoring
for position

just another
pair of feet
trying to get
away
from the
last
finish
line

Separated At A Still Birth Of A Nation

the children of the pimp and ho
generation
dizzy from the centrifugal forces
the new dawn has lit upon
their smiling faces
of death
realize this much:
the conveniences of being from the
criminal class
far outweigh the consequences
unless, of course
you are met with the sudden conviction
lest ye be judged
as you have judged
because
money never judges money
all that harshly
but poverty is an eternal bully
that blinded justice
on the playground
when they were
just kids
on saddleback dinosaurs
come, doctor, do tell
is that more exotic smoke you have brought forth?
is it on the menu for delivery or inclub consumption?
it sells best if it isn't a bestseller
even though, selling isn't everything
but, the list in the times is still something jerks jack off to
the troglodytes have sent us back
to the korea we never left alone
the trembling is ignored in atheistic foxholes
the grunting is heard from Palineotologist trenches
dug in so deep they could not work the stolen
parts on the centrifuge that made up the forest

enriching all the hiroshima wet dreams that ran down
the insides of quivering thighs in angst ridden unicorn .jpegs
that are thumbnails of pretty moments in rice milk diplomacy
while the industrial revolution is still turning
behind everyone's backs like a spinning knife wound
discovered to be an ancient javelin thrown as a game
that turned into a war overnight overland oversea oversee
overall
shells rained down from heaven before the sun could make it
up
rise and shine in the land of the rising sun until its lights out
these shells are less sea and less see and more big blast
all along the parallel as the electric sounds of uranium
drive the turbines that turn the tables on who will be next
in the musical chair game of world domination
that has been dumbing down the syndrome
until the muck raked 60 years ago
comes floating to the top most point of no return
then
and only then
it is asked of the lord of the skies adorned
with mushroom light shows that make the kids say "WOW!!!"
again and again
please forgive us that can't forgive ourselves for not giving the
rest
of the world a second chance after we gambled the first one
away
in a solid show of force between ancient fellowships both
north and south, east and west
let us pray
lettuce spray
it makes no difference, either way
let them all eat fast food cabbages
tiny microscopes see tiny possibilities
the details of it in the intricacies in sound and movement...

a frantic squeeze...

then *"POP"*!!!

there are no more

weasels

left to go...

As Short As I Could Reckon In Time
for Mike Taylor and E.A. Poe

in search of el dorado up in mighty colorado
el conquistador has fallen off his steed
his rusty armor holds him back
the misery of failure holds him down
angels that once blessed his path,
now gone, they are not felt in his heart
as the cold wins its place there
bringing his journey to an end
his lust for golden churches fails him
his desire for redemption so faraway from Spain
is the last prayer he mutters across his frostbitten lips
he dies a mile high in a valley full of frozen tears
if only he had a poem to keep him safe from icy oblivion
he visited here too closed minded and early
to read the words of los desperados
to let those words warm his congested heartlessness
these words of humbler beginnings born in mountain shacks
spewed out next to fallen amusement parks in a world that
misplaced the golden spanish churches of ol' colorado
these words that would heal the wild thing imprisoned
these words that would save the souless vagabonds of war
these words that would free the reins of wild horses
descendents of a lost spaniard's battle steed
their blood the bare mestizo of time & consequences
these words freed them to let them stampede through the
wilderness
loping up to mountaintops high above
to scream out for freedom
against a backdrop of tattered flags
murder no longer their bargain
they scream it out in whispers
like it has never been screamed before
it may take the world too long to hear it
like it took el conquistador too long to die

in that long ago forsaken winter of regrets
but, what you don't hear will never give you comfort
& what you do hear, you will never be able to unhear
never ever again, so scream for your freedom
let go of all that is weighted down with gold & false promise
let the horse run away, let it stampede with what is wild
let the stampede be the thunder that
is the rhythm you will live by forever or at least today
or at the very least until a tomorrow
that may never come for you, anyway

Chupa

i am inside a lil' piece of you that
at the velocity of life
as it is in the living
what has been made
as it is in the making
as you encounter those
who are searching for
something to create an
instantaneous and artificially
organic moment with
a catalyst for
immediate analysis
something to apply fire to
that will instantly alter the
conscious moment
forever
from rock to oil to smoke to gas and
finally back to crystalline formations
on the inner folds of a young
crack whore's damaged lungs, she coughs
up blood and offers it up as love
her blackened fingers are the
venus sculptures missing limbs

her womb gives birth

to pregnant expectations,

crack baby needs

South Of No North

when the border gets lonely
it begs to be crossed
under cover of darkness
through blistered landscapes
hearts beat strongest
when they move out
into the unknown
looking for something
that looks like a dream
the eyes settle for glory
that can break any heart
in the next broken beat

Drawn & Quartered

like a little albino rabbit
hiding in the snow
the pink eyes
giving away
the hiding
like little
laser
beacons

like a flower petal shaped as a dragon's wing
hidden in the pages of a forgotten book
opened in the musty depths
of a lost used book store
crumbled at the touch
of anxious fingertips
before the beauty
could be memorized
one last time

like a cancer that is undetectable
hidden in stasis for so long
until it is malignant
actively killing
beyond
treatment

like a matador in training
lost his heart to the horn
of the resistant bull
fearing what is lost
not what was gained
leaving the shoe
behind
on the ritual
sand

covered in blood

as these four pieces spread to points
of opposite compass
they give flight to fancy
somewhat
like an idea in the mind that tells on itself
with an eternal question never answered
"if this is not really freedom, then what is?"
it grows in patterns of equal doubt
equal compassion
equal guilt
equal love
until it is almost found
on a deathbed or
just before an accidental
disaster
that we all saw coming
without ever looking
for any sign
of it
before it happens

Life In A Holiday

it all can be so
fleeting, so taken for granted
like teeth that seem healthy
that get knocked loose in a
torrent of blood, spit and drama
it can all be so expansive
like the feelings that seem
to come from nowhere and side swipe laughter
and undermine love, which has its parameters for expansion
but falls without a strong foundation

it can all be so small and insignificant
like a look or a glance between
two passing strangers and the thought
later on in life that you missed something back there
somewhere

it can all be so powerful and so diminished
all at once, in the same moment
like the hammer come down with
a thunderous silence that is still and calm
at the point of impact

at the place of collision

nothing moves in that moment
nothing gives way to universal
law of attracting opposites or
motion causing motion

there is just a stillness without violence

yet the power of a mighty anvil is present
beneath a great hammerhead
that is pounding out life
with a vigorous beat

that stifles time and calms the broiling turmoil
of memory and regret
                    as the hammerhead rises
a tiny vacuum is made into pocket of love that smiles
                    through the sheet of pain and fear
                    that smells like ancient metallurgy
exploding into
worked fragments that
block organic sensations and emotions

you fight to get to that point of impact
your whole life in secretive struggle
only to place it all against the forged surface
only to anticipate the blows of an unrelenting force
            older than all pasts and vast as all futures
            incomprehensible as it may seem before the
            moment strikes its mark, it is nonetheless
            a moment of hope that is both powerful
            & silent amid all the noise and collapse

                    of this life
                            in this world

Sick In The Sun

for a long time there was cold
hours into days into months
sickness came into our body
but, today the rays of heat
wash us into hopeful play as
the sun beats up the senses
makes the heart forget ice
feelings melt into slush
lungs remember with
constricted love
lost inside alveoli
that swell with hurt pride
no coughing consoles these broken breaths
taken on tuberculine cues from blue eyed skies
they don't want to be the organ that forgets
they know the folly of the body in love
the cold always comes back
no matter where the sunshine
comes from today
the new heat will falsely disrobe us
leave us naked in embrace
ignorant of the icy tendrils
waiting to overcome our body
in the vulnerable night of changing weather
this most fickle time of year

Homeless

you can never go home
once you leave
you can never go back
to where you were
if you leave for too long
if you leave too soon
if you leave your hat
hanging up back there
it ain't home no more
someone might be
wearing that hat
by the time you
make it back
everything changes
and if you stay home
without ever leaving
it might change anyway
so always be ready
for the potential
for a new hat
for a new home
you can always find them
sometimes they are as close
as just around the corner
sometimes it can take years and miles
and you will still be searching
without ever finding a hat that fits nicely
or a home that you can call your own
but you will find family
along the way
everywhere
even if you never
find a home again
that is the best part of love
that has ever been found

by those that searched for it
even when they couldn't find a home

Street Corner With No Calvary In Sight

the sound catches wind as it blows down the barren street
it rises and falls like an unplanned symphony of sighs
punctuated by freeway traffic in the distance
drifting in and out of its volume as eyes
try to focus through blurring cold
not too cold, not as cold as it
can get in other parts of
the world, where
steel is hidden
under snow
a white
blanket
that covers
everything with
a shimmering mirage
that seems so mystic as it
glistens in the moonlight of
distant daydreams that take me
away from here for a moment that
I need to know its not so bad right now
feeling the missing and the heartaches of
years gone by while I lose my eyesight on this
lonely street corner as people all over the world
suffer a little more than me in increments that can be
measured by world news and body counts piling high in
adverse reaction to the hope some keep close in their hearts
that it will get better, maybe not today, maybe some day,
maybe

Mink Coat on Skid Row

he was the prince of poverty
rarely left his area
his hood
she was a transplanted
duchess
they met on a corner
that was perfumed
with layered stench
and the lowest
economy
she spoke of dreams
and castles that she
was waiting for a calling
back to
a beckoning from a
lost family inheritance
that would save them both
he bought into for a moment
because he had to know what
the story was
the ostentatious wardrobe and
the air of dignity that cloaked
the obvious insanity
was impossible to resist
on an unseasonably hot day
where the shuffle from soup kitchen
to dumpster diving
to recycling center
to liquor store
to shady spot
was the same
as it always was
until she stepped out
on that corner and
displayed her semi-conscious
soul for everyone to see

only 6th and San Pedro
was not impressed
and even he got tired
as he looked in her eyes
for a long moment
and sadly realized
that no one was home
and there was shuffles
and slides left to make
before the street lights would
take over the saddest watch of the day
and a mink coat might not seem
so crazy come past midnight
he looked for her, and wondered
but never saw her again
she had been just a
moment
of distraction
in a world that demanded
a balance between sustenance
and medication of an
illness no doctor can
cure

More Tickle, Less Slap

love never reveals
the sweetest part
until there is a
certain distance
that is not a
measurement
but instead
the age old
predicament

how much more
of this?

how much less
of that?

you get what you get
you want what you want

deprivation kinks always
have it easiest
the slightest touch
every so often
is all they need

satiated desires can
trigger depression
in most cases

is that all there is?
is this as good as its gonna get?
is this the last time
we will ever feel
this way again?

if its too hard now

don't worry
it will be softer
soon
nothing stays consistent
in love
if it gets too soft
you will feel the
most pain
because it won't
travel the distance
or make up the
time difference
if it is barely heard
barely felt
if it becomes too
much to bare
across a
barren
landscape
with words dangling
in the distance
like discarded
skeletal remains
not a missing link
enough to be
preserved in history
forever

this thunder is life
this violence in the
synapse is necessary
to sustain a flow
a distant connection
that is always in flux
until you nail it down
with the wiggle
of a feather

Ride Til I Die

getting ready to drive home
after a night of work
doesn't seem worth much
its not enough to make much difference
or make a dent in any struggle
the car is on the edge
one headlight
no insurance
driver's license
about to
expire
crack here
leak there
broken this
malfunctioned that
bald tires with nails in them
waiting to sound off at the most inopportune moment
the guy pushing the cart collecting bottles and cans
out of the garbage strewn street
is looking at me
as I look at him
"at least you got a car"
he says to break the silence
I look at the cart and it takes me back
I remember how itchy the same clothes get
especially the underwear
after a month of continuous wear
how the socks get so unbearable and stiffened
in moments
only to be sticky sweet and rancid smelling
moments after walking again
walking in shoes that are deteriorating off of
rotting feet that ache and stink
walking to look for cans, bottles, change, unfinished food
laid on top of garbage bins

looking for it until
you rummage deeper
if you find nothing
the burning stomach
the weakened mind
looks for easy pickins
something petty to steal
if nothing petty is around
it can immediately
become more grand
inside a fractured mind
covered in matted hair
locks of dread
that are packed inside
a knit watch cap
for the cold winter
coming out like a cascade
of wooly beaver tails
with no hope of untangling
you walk away from all the convention
this world has to offer
in complete anger and frustration
because you see no hope
for this situation to ever change
something has to give
at some point
these memories are not my favorite
or my most proud
never wanted it to come this again
but the next stop on the line seems to be
my least favorite exit
this is as far as my ticket gets me
as we are pulling into the station
of the last destination
on a long ride to nowhere

Calle de Embarcadero

along a cold winter brook that runs out to an awaiting lagoon
as the lagoon wants for tidal changes to empty it into the sea
thoughts and feelings spit out onto the shallow surface
of the moving water as it rolls along with tear-like raindrops
causing ripples in its current that bellow out into each other
under chilled winter skies colliding with steep mountain vistas
that turn gunmetal grayness into moody cloak of lonely
wanting

the heart is sickly the mind is sickly the body is sickly
all in unanimous condition with the weather and the
surroundings
ambling in and out of hurt and comfort the same way the brook
veers in and around the tidal marsh while snowy egrets glide
through fingers of mist that rise up in random columns
to touch the underneath of their brilliant wings so softly

the sound of pounding surf in the distance
is like war drums coming near
what will there be to fight this time around?
what alliance will falter or be newly made?
questions that can't be answered by stumbled feet
or broken prayers in quiet meditation
as the waters keep flowing by
keep falling down
keep freezing up
down into swollen throat
filling tattered lungs with icy resentments
that search for bits of warmth
to melt it all back down into a love
that is only momentary at best

it is that time of year here
it s the place this is
this is that part of this journey

102

holding up a frailness
hoping no one sees
until the fever passes

Fires We Have Known

choking for love
and recognition

breathing for life
and survival

blowing on the
embers like a
rogue wind
named Santa Ana

mushrooms of smoke
cascade from your
open mouth and
flared nostrils
converting your words
to shooting sparks
that ignite a conflagration
of ghosts and martyrs

walk this path naked
across Mulholland Dr.
out into the vistas of
the darkness that is
punctuated in the
distance by red eyed
beacons of flame that
leapt into the underbrush
ready to burn like an ancient
sacrament of ritual that frees
the spirit and soars above the
flames of homes built in canyons
that run dry as the wind

the panorama is bright lights

above charcoal ruins

love is ash and embers
reduced to this
by times passing

it burns every
year like a pyreal
calendar for lost
souls that kiss the
walls of hell with
licking flames
that tell the tale
of what has passed
as the new crop
of flammable material
grows inside the remains
of blazing desires that
have been extinguished
by loss of time

loss of shelter

loss of life

loss of cooling

winds of calm
that are waiting
to blow once
again as the
autumn nears
and the exposed
ravines beg to be
made into rivers
of muddy water
through riverbeds
of broken concrete

toward an unforgiving
ocean of lost desires

Haunted On The B Train

for Skylita

somewhere on the train underneath chinatown
a smile travels too fast away from here
uptown bound until downtown frowns
come back, with the eyes that lighten up
come back, with the soft sound of the wind
inside every breath before and every word after
the tracks rattle rhythm to the circulatory pulse pounding away

what good are arms that forget what embrace felt like?
what good are legs that never tangle and weave like tapestry?
what good are soft memories of when we were near to being?

the train keeps its destinations intact never ever running out of
track
somewhere on the train underneath chinatown
a ticket is missing a ride as a station never misses one less rider
feet bustling around all day below traffic hustling all night
above
time stands still for the longest of all loves as they pass each
other like
planets in distant solar systems never seeing each other in orbit
but feeling the pull of life's gravity in the middle axis of love
falling into the darkest part of your eyes as the tunnels go black
somewhere on the train underneath chinatown

107

by all accounts

she pushes numbers
next to words
to get an equation
that makes sense
of it all
it gets close
like happiness
but never
manifests
so its more
like disappointment
the song of the word
as it passes through
the metaphysical and
transforms the physical
suspends times and places

like this moment here
that became aligned
with a grateful child

she sings out
at the awakening
and the wake

a beautiful song
of announcement
and mourning
all at once that
she has taught
herself

all senses rendered here
unto her
this little ball of hope
whistling through

missing teeth
as she captures
life away from
turning pages

it is always true
that as long as
a mouth moves it out
and a hand sets it down
we will be here

together

Down On Bruno St.
For Father G and all the homeboys & girls

these cobblestones are seldom looked at
this dust is new but blows like it is old

school is a memory that is held down
written on the pages of text books
that are handed out like precious
metal chained to a desire for a
freedom like you never knew

freedom like you are not sure
what that could mean to you
stubbing toes as you shuffle
across the dusty old bricks
trying to walk tall and cool

cool ain't happening today
as the sun beats down on
a drink of water that is like
a mirage hanging above the
concrete riversides a little more
than a block away and below from
the conversation with the detectives
about the homey that is hanging on by
a thread to a delicate life support after the
weekend shooting at the seven eleven left him
bleeding out of his head wound that was like an
unfiltered portal into a world that has been at war
in so many forms for so many years that the detective
breaks eye contact after he admits he doesn't know who
to hold responsible yet this time because it just doesn't make
sense to kill hope on a night when people are looking forward
to celebrating life even though we all fear the reaper verdugo
as the black form in the shadows that cuts us down when we
least expect it bringing a harvest of grieving tears with

haunting moans that punctuate the darkness like
stilletto stars walking away in make-up with the
most broken heart east of glendale blvd. as
the stars fade into the railroad ties that run
along the boundary between one hood or
another hood like a steel zipper that
can't keep out the flies on the faces
of the bodies that have piled up
over the years into a temple
that towers above all the
streets and the heights

standing so high it
towers above the
fragile peace
falls away
into a faint
echo of an
infant's cries
as it is welcomed
into this world of
desert parks, towns,
ravines and reservoirs
that hold all the tears
cried over all the fallen
as the war cry is something
everyone claims they got used to
a long time ago
before the first forever
was even recorded
on the first wall

already a promise of apricots betrayed

burst out before spring
leap out of winter coats
now useless, now what

soon to travel far away
delicate petals on wind
floating far from home

pollinated dreams fly
upward so lightly on
announcing harvest
without humility of
loss

attracting bees with
no sense of season
just a purpose that
begets a moment
full of hope

small fertility starting
under misguided sun
left alone to die for
a predatory moon

a voice came early
like a fragrant call
this year,
announcing it all
like a delicate trumpeter
telling us to wait for nothing
except what truly matters most

Letter From Pelican Bay

How you doin', bro?
it has been 30 years today
since we last spoke words
full of bravado, calo & chisme
waiting on different buses
to take us away from tehachapi

seems like I been here since then
just doing my job
getting myself moved deeper
into this beast's belly
every moment that goes by

I lost most of my hair & teeth by now
I lost my appendix, too
not really missing much of it
anymore
I tried to hang in the hunger strike
but, they forced me back to life
so I don't call people "holmes" much
anymore
it started sounding fake as my teeth
plus, the c.o.'s try to talk like me
so I had to change it up
thought that might make you smile
cuz of the way you used to say
"we got to be ready always
to change it up on these fools"
you used to say that
when we were youngsters
all the time
I remember
still

for reals, tho

everyone here cries in their cell
everyone here regrets something
but, don't ever get to talk about it
only the walls & pillows hear me

while you went in & out
running free finally
I stayed here
for 30 years
until today
don't know how many more days
either one of us got left breathing
but, we made it this far together
even though we have been
so far apart

don't ever forget me, carnale
I won't ever forget you
we ain't kids no more
for reals, tho

I had a dream you became a priest
just to get a visit
just to bring me
a pack of smokes
so, in closing
I wanted to keep it real
don't become a priest
on my account
I quit smoking
over a year ago

Armed Struggle

intoxicated by meaning
drunk on wayward emotions
bullets meant to warn
hit right between the eyes
knives meant to pierce hearts
open letters of foreclosure
bombs dropped from drones
in order to humble fanatics
into a quick surrender
before the holy holiday celebrations
begin with a commercial fervor
these bombs, some work, some don't
these bombs, dropped ordinance
become improvised devices
that send packages of dead children
back home from far away
instead of certain victory
sobered now by meaninglessness
looking into gaunt future landscapes
still intent to carry burdens up the hill
to place them on the altar
to forget their purpose
to forget their weight
to avoid the consequence
at all costs if only the price
would make it possible
the payment is coming due on everything
until the machines that print money
are broken down to be used
as weapons or plowshares
these choices will be easier
in the final moment
with the limited options
as it stands now
we have the freedom to choose

more than we can handle
in this forsaken moment
of eternal quandary
over the basics
under all the complications
of a kevlar culture
dying from a chest wound
in utter amazement
at its own fragility
beneath its best armor
even with these arms
it can no longer reach
its own bleeding heart

Hard Times

the hardest times were not the moments
of terror as a child in a world too
overwhelming with fear to be
faced alone without some
form of release that
the child knows
is wrong

the hardest times were not the moments
when the LAPD came in the early morning
shooting your favorite dog as she slept
on the back porch before kicking in
the doors of a dilapidated beach bungalow
or the NYPD on horseback during a riot
that they started and finished by breaking
2 of your ribs and leaving you in the tombs
for 34 days without due process
or the SFPD waking you up with swinging batons
as you slept in a muni tunnel to get out
of the cold fog at night
or the Iowa state troopers beating you into a puddle
of your own piss that you couldn't hold
in your bladder any longer

the hardest times were not the moments
where you left children behind in uncertainty
lost touch with where they were
seeing them only briefly
burying one of them at 9
never finding the oldest one again
sending letters to your son from prison
missing out on all those lives
for so many years

the hardest times were not the moments
lost in a taiwanese nightmare with no sleep

117

held captive in a thai prison
captured by federales in baja
hiding in a ditch as paramilitaries
searched for you nearby
in ancient Chiapas
or further south in Brasilia
fighting bare knuckled
just to earn the right
to walk out of a favela alive

the hardest times were not the moments
friends, family and lovers died and took
a piece of you away with them, never
to return
or the time your body finally turned against you
organs failing due to toxic abuse and disease
as the doctors wrote you off as another
bleak, uninsured statistic
or all the brokenhearted, impoverished moments
with no shelter or love or friendship left
with no hope of ever making it back
with nothing left to lose

no, none of these

the hardest times have proved to be the moments
where you have worked your way back into a place
where there may be a chance at a new life
a hope for a different future than what
you had accepted as your dismal fate
so long ago
and you have to have faith that you will make it
even though you see the world as really nothing more
than just a bunch of hard times that you have known it to be

these moments are the hardest times of all
where the ether of faith escapes me

Blue

On a sunny day at the car wash on the corner of Sunset and Alvarado my wife and I were waiting for our shiny black car to be done with its washing and waxing. She was happy and bouncy as the sunlight danced off of her bleached blond hair that had a flash of purple highlight dazzling the air at the back of her neck. The way she styled her hair drew attention to the color contrast that seemed to even match her Chloe sunglasses. Her smile infected me with this invincible feeling that I could not be stopped by anything. Her smile glowed and my buzz was right with it. I wanted it to be this way forever. I ordered some tacos and cokes from the taco stand and we sat down at the plastic tables to eat while our car was being wheeled out to the hand drying, detailing area. Some salsa spilled on my new shirt, that matched my hat, while I was eating.

I let it get to me right away and my whole mood changed. She laughed, as I became angry, and she told me the shirt really brought out the blue in my eyes as she dabbed at it with a bandana.

I was too pissed off to notice the compliment.

I still regret not letting that moment be happy, but I was too stressed out about a stain on a Dodger jersey when love was right there, trying to touch my heart.

In Trying To Keep Up with Basho

walking along a path with no end
that can be seen in the distance
looking up ahead or back to where
the journey had begun

walking along this path to walk
for the very sake of walking
in & of itself, as the path
will take us along

walking & walking as each step
is different from the last
as long as it never steps
where the last foot fell
before it stepped here

notice this apart from walking
the world moves around us
as we move around the world
it was never meant to mean
more than that

it was the meaning of it all
all along

this place we are going
this path we are walking
this is what it is all about
the secrets are just lies
we tell ourselves
to make the journey
more exciting
as we distract our sight
from the real excitement
of the world around us

living & breathing
same as us
until we notice the similar
way in which
we can excite the world
by walking with purpose
giving & taking along the way
walking & walking for the sake
of the walk that never ends
on the path that is never ending
as long as that is the path we have chosen
as long as that is the path that has chosen us

Gutted

split wide open
from star to stern
from rooter to tooter
opening the portal for it all
to come spilling outward in a deluge
of all things both sacred & vile
& all of it in between the two
all thrown together by the violence
all tossed down as one
& when that spring
has come unsprung
you know it will never go back
inside itself the same way again
& you learn that per diem
is not just an allowance
for a day
but, an increment of time
& you know that all the time you have left
can be told like a fortune or seen like a future vision
all according to how your guts look
laying on the ground
in front of you
as you stare
vacantly
for the moment
at the parts of the sum
never to be the sum of parts
ever again
& that is a moment of most amazing wonder
when that is all you will really know for certain
& it will be all you will ever really need to know
forever

If You Make It To The Sally Port

notches made in haste not waste not fashion
a weapon fashioned out of odds and ends
keep the angle close to the chest
keep the arc close to the neck
flurry after flurry
fight for your life
all eyes upon everyone here
scratches on the walls mark the days
segregated by the administration of healing
some say it will heal you if you live through it
most do live, but what dies? when and where does it give in?
what flies away in well lit moments of hopelessness among the
lost?
what comes home to roost in the darkened corners of every
turn here?
its not what you think, its not that it wasn't made to sound like
a form
of redemption you might have missed along the way to the
forum as
chariots sidetracked down blind alleyways paved with broken
bones
penance required for time sentenced, served, paroled out and
away
as long as it was meant to be endured like a burning pain under
raw skin
that fits too tight in every dark corner where someone is always
watching
even when you look in the mirror there is someone checking up
on you
better make sure you have the proper front in place like your
own
personal sociopathic loin cloth that makes you king shit of no
man's land
just cells of life joined to dying cells that meant no harm as
children

as they once laughed and played in inner recesses of broken
brain daydreams
skipping away over sunlit hilltops for two into the echoing
distance
as the reality of these echoing walls filled with conversations
that mask
murderous fears forming into gangs of swarming violence at
the ready
one false move is all it takes as you think of love with the
sounds of toilets
flushing   you think of welcome home days with screaming
fits of delusion
bouncing around your head like crowns of thorns   you think
of lovers you
know in truth you will never hold again as the ancient sounds
of misguided
lust intruding as power given or power taken away drift
through the stinging
air of the sharpened night as terror places its wreath at your feet
as people who
feel the most righteous of any in the land (as most seem to do)
tell their children
about the healing place they sent all the men that deserved it to
  to make up for what
they did so long ago to make this place a safer place to get
them out of they way that
seems to not care enough to join the ranks of what was given as
order as they break inside
only to share the break with you   or you   or you when we
meet outside the moment that
all was lost in the losing of the human feeling of the connection
of the bargain as it all went
south and the chips feel where they may as ten days straight in
leg irons will make you
abide by the rifles held over head and all the walls point in the
same direction here

and all the iron sings like wild banshees loosed from hells
grasp singing with metallic
throats that deride all the moments that tear the thoughts of
what peace used to mean
in the twisting of time in the bending of mind that folds in on
the heart and has so little
to do with the soul on ice as it is said about this life in the
cooler   in the warehouse of
humanity lost for all the things they did now that they wonder
little about all they
have done that they were never caught for   never cared
for   never loved for
it's a never never land if you never make it out of here   you
have to move on it
like it's the only chance you will ever get if you do   make
it out of here, somehow

The Difference Between Free and Freedom

to walk on the playground
as a naive child looking for love
you had to take an ass whooping
just to get playtime started

firecrackers from tijuana were as illegal
as all the housekeepers, dishwashers and fruit pickers
that lived in the trailer park shanty of the wash
but, sales by the brick could earn money
for a summer shackled by poverty

the example was set in stone somewhere
it seemed that infallible and permanent
play sports to get out of here
join the marine corps to get out if that failed
risk your life and imprisonment if those choices failed
huff glue, get tattooed, fight for the hood til you die
if you just have no ambition to leave here

if you left on your own you would most surely
spend moments alone in quiet places that exist
between bedlam and chaos, horror and sacrifice
listening to the story of your genetics told there
in silent whispers of doubted facts and fairy tales
the codes so overlapped and mixed up
there would be no clear allegiance
ever pledged to anything more
than simple survival
dug out of dark
concrete corners

run for your life now and again
as long as life will have you
run to the ocean sides
to the redwood forests

across the fruited plains
over purple mountains
standing truly majestic
over runaway vistas

hope might live over every horizon
might be pursued in every direction

evade detection by armed and dangerous
authorities waving flags on the sleeves
every moment until you are burned alive
by your own vigilance inside spoons
inside small pipes of your own ingenious
makings

avoid extinction by living on the inside
far more than it showed on the outside

roll it up, ball it up, give it up
over and over and over again
to the trauma and the pain
the turmoil and the chains
your back breaks under the weight
of the work you were never promised
in this promised land that was promised
to someone else and their children and
their grand children and so on until
you realize that the reservations are too real
to ever go away and the history books just say
whatever
so smugly in the face of petrified tears
that you realize the mother of all
realizations

this land is like the playground
where you were first forced to fight
against your will

when all you wanted was to play
for a moment
but, that moment never came
and if it did
you missed it
so now you miss the point
of the celebration as well

there are people that are
missing things
there are people that have
found things
there are people that are
wanting things

I have been all three
but, this was never freedom
                              for me

Picasso Doesn't Do Much For Her

it is from across rooms of perspective
inside twisted chambers of the mind
her face like spoon fed butter scoops
dripping past eyes elongating into noses
her body like turning angles becoming blocks
building out the fantasy play of light upon shadow
her angular teeth grip a thorny rose that pricks her
head bent upon squared neck dropping to buttocks
separating cleavage from fish and beach with ball in play
with ball in motion as dance is kinetic to abuse of love
of self of indulgence of grandiose scale of cognac
of absinthe of blue moods against green vengeance
with disfigured fairy tales morphing into lost vistas
never seen by the eye of an old woman's cataracts
hardly felt inside the bronzed goat vaginal walls
as war rages outside on the inside all the time
it is injustice, all of it, from the fly in the ointment
to the napalm dropped on mama and babe innocence
the contorted eyes of terror open mouthed kissing
death as if embrace were only meant for mistress
as wives got the loneliness of it all in cascades
of flamenco bulls running into matadors on bloody hooved
sand
written off as salon after salon becomes meaningless pedigree
as if the wisdom of castles had left anything less than magic
for the love, for the woman, for the light etching contrast
into prism into lust into temper into explosion into work
it all falls away into emotions left like a high water mark
into a lifetime of perspective reaching out for a better
point of view against an overrated misunderstanding
these balls are made of brass to last a little longer
not really so much beautiful as useful to angels
gone blind and now they feel their way back to heaven
alone, how every saint must feel in silent visage
waiting for it all to come back together again

just lay down naked on the bed in the
morning sunlight as it comes through
the bedroom window
I want to see you for who you are
less clearly

Thanksgiving Day Sans Something

Captain John Smith is retired now
he hides in the phone book
among many John Smiths
just like him

He never married Pocahontas
because that takes the fun
out of raping heathens
that wear pretty jewels
far away from home
it is more exotic
without marital
consent

Walt Disney wants the story line to be
always as wholesome as possible
from his liquid nitrogen throne
he changes history the way
a pilgrim never had to
their rhythm was so
natural that their
race would be
pure forever

this corn is so hybrid it makes injuns sick
ain't that a kick in the pants with a
dirty moccasin foot
ha ha ha
this pumpkin pie
is frozen like
Uncle Walt's
head

it is not made from scratch
like mom used to bake

131

this turkey has tryptophan
enhanced by Afghan opium poppies
so the next tax cut will help defense spending
along with the black market promises that were made
to guarantee a slower escalation before Christmas
so we can all see those reruns of the halftime show
that were animated back in the sixties when
Suess was still a doctor trying to fix the
broken hearts and warped minds of scared children
he retired a broken hearted man with a warped rhyme
Pocahontas only gets married in animation
in real life she is on a res waiting for a casino check
that has nothing to do with
what John Smith did to her
or pilgrims sharing
blankets of a dying
fever
She cries when Burl Ives sings along
to his banjo by the by

remember,
your purchasing power is necessary this Friday
to start the chorus out right
"every little thing is gonna be all..."
quickly changing into
"I gave you everything I got for a lil' piece of mind"

there are many many pieces on this occasion
but, no one seems to mind
even the soup kitchens
are full of festive
movie stars

the pilgrims knew
these are savages and we must make it through this winter

no matter what

god spoke that day in a verse
of pox and cannon fire

it is all so convenient now

let the parade
begin

Thanksgiving Day With Something

I have to be grateful every day
my life depends on it
people that care about me
deserve my gratitude
I am working on life
all the time
every day has to be thanksgiving
without the turkey and pumpkin pie
or the stories of conquered people
beguiled into helping the people
who will take everything away
then being told to be grateful
that you survived this long
to see the party that they
are throwing every day
to honor the war of
attrition that I lost
before I was born
even though
surviving might not be winning
it still might be everything
except for the moments
it is a lonely shell
playing a game
you know all
the rules to
or at least
you get to make them up as we go
I have to be grateful to follow them

I have to be grateful every day
my life depends on it

Brush

seen in dreams
bristled attempts
at past
resolution

fingers pulled through
the tangled mane
that now
tangles
on its loneliness

care must be taken
to keep straight
the stranded
moments

pulling down the motion
top to bottom
as it stands
silent

culling away the bad moon
clouding the last words
tear drops sprayed
away in mist

shouldered burdens grow
gaining a momentum
the pendulum
falls back

the eyes see once again
for an instance before
stylized guess work

look away into
what was taken
look back into
obscurity

future
mirrored
times
ticking
one by
one
out of
pocket

full of hope
sunbeams
fruit stands
ocean waves
just beyond
the wind blown
beaches of
broken
hearts
held in
jelly
wishes

Out There

facing the sting of the air stream
racing through an open wound
Nina sings to me about prayers
I been a sinner man so long
there are no more words
that the heavens would hear
from my blistered lips
that never learned
to beg for you
properly

Drowning In The Shallow End

sometimes you accidentally pluck a nose hair
that is so painfully rooted in your soul
it triggers a cascade of everything
rolling down inside your brow

the suicides of all the years past
run behind the droopy eyelids
like a back lit paper puppet parade
projected against the soft curtains
of a gutted and languishing soul
like it had become an opium den
on the wrong side of the burmese border
danger always veiled by the painless smoke
coursing through the determined veins

the first responders arrive upon the scene
they appraise they are not qualified for this
the radio news crackles up all the vision
the report is stark and familiar

no one knows exactly how to reach the lost souls
that have waded into the dark waters all alone
knee deep in the last hysteria of living
the boat has been sent out in vain
the dangling life rants out loud
just out of reach of a rescue
that stands by in awe
as the bystanders
gape wide in the
paralyzed
spectacle
of trauma

the helicopter arrives in flutters of angels wings above
high above circling above too late above

last words are just air bubbles gone inaudible
last rites are left to callers of talk radio responsibility
always present in america to right the ship with post-mortem
analysis

I now notice that traffic is thinning somewhat like my anemic
blood
I get to work and say my prayers in a silent, godless world
of elocuted commerce without grace
we don't save lives here
they save themselves or perish
bottom line

I walk into a solemn chaos
we all know there is one less of us
as we look around the fluorescent room
and I remember what my granpa said to me when I was 4 years
old
"not all the puppies make it" were his words that I have held on
to
not all the puppies, indeed
especially the ones that see
parades across their eyelids
parades they may join without
any self control
once the last piece of hope drifts by
then drifts away with a beckoning lure
that can draw a lost soul into a walk upon the water
one last chance at a rescue that might never happen

Reglas

if I lead, follow me
if I stumble, help me
if they kill me, avenge me
if I am a traitor, kill me

Trying To Fit In As A Square Peg In A Round World

fuck this shit
it just don't work for me
this working for scraps and crumbs
while people laugh at you
in that anemic "hahahahaha"
being humble for opportunities
hoping for the best
having faith in good works
humility is its own reward
I am told, by a straight face
"you are just a late bloomer at this.
you'll get it one day soon."
piety is its own reward
where is the piss and the blood and the cum in this?
where is the last bit of heart
being put to the test in this?
braver people than I could ever be
created this polite society for me
but, I rejected it all
in favor of running fear races
to see who could reach scary finish lines first
or die trying
cuz trying don't mean shit
unless you die doing it
fuck this mealy mouthed attempt
to force pegs into slots that accommodate
hard corners that stop these stones
from rolling along
crushing the green blood out of moss
as it gives way underneath
this rock rolls, baby
rolling all night long
looking for round holes
in order to remove any corners
that being a square for a moment

might have etched into my hide
like bad algorithmic tattoos
inside my softened eyelids
and scar tissue from paper cuts
received at poetry workshops
along with a hangnail
from changing the cd player
one motivational speaker
to the next
I need a lot of dope
a couple of diseased whores
and a good bar fight
all padded by some ill gotten gains
in my dirty deep pockets
just to feel clean again

Loosing My Grip More And More

mama said if I didn't change
something bad was gonna happen to me
she was always trying to warn me
but, I was always thinking
"so what? bring it on, get it over with!" to myself
not because of bravery or courage
not because I had it all figured out
not anything against mama, either
the time keeps going by as I hang on best that I can
sometimes I am not hanging on for shit_
sometimes hanging loses its meaning loses its purpose
what's the point of hanging on when you feel like that no
matter what?
what's the point of hanging on to life if all of life is just
hanging on?
what's the point of hanging on so long to the frayed out ends of
burned out dreams that never had a chance anyways?
what's the point of hanging on to the remnants of love
that don't match up into anything much useful anymore?
what;s the point of hanging on to the last pieces of shattered
soul
that are the dirty, used up fragments of something so forgotten
it can never be remembered again?
there is not a lot of hope for equanimity anymore
there is less hope for anything as the hanging continues day by
day
hope can be so illusory as everything begins to weaken
all the time that transpires can feel wasted on the useless effort
I can see what it looks like in the mended life of others
who seem to have reasons to pull together to be together
for reasons I don't understand so easily anymore
who seem to have abundant hope for the future
who seem to have had a taste of something
unknown in my hungry life in my hungry soul
which just seems to leave me with

nothing left to smoke with no desire to smoke anyway
nothing left to drink that works on this hollowness anymore
nothing left to dream when the echo rattles the empty insides
nothing left to do in moments that turn to hours that turn to
days
nothing but watching a whole lifetime
take the longest wrong turn for the worst out of control crash
landing
mama told me long ago when I was young so I can't say I was
never warned
there is not a lot left to do here except for hanging on
to the end of this long rope
that I was born hanging on to
too long ago to be saved by it much longer

Haphazard Machine World

laying out the words as the noon whistle blows
in the forlorn distances far away from here
using the machine as much as the machine
is using me to make machine made lines
in the well oiled sand of the machine
as the coffee brews too wicked in the little
institutional coffee machine
I always prefer to make coffee slow
and inefficient dripping hot water through a sock
the older the sock the better, long stained from
years of coffee grounds rubbed into the cotton
until it is thick with irredeemable lost nights of sleeplessness
until it is blackened with the build up of years of broken
backed laborers stooping with cramped hands to cultivate
that brewed cup that is now so bitter from the plastic and alloy
of this tiny machine that spurts and belches as if it had some
important proposition to make on my haphazard late start
of my haphazard late life existence with bitter grounds for
divorce from the romantic notion that I am impervious to
all this movement around me that I once fought tooth and nail
until I became toothless skinless spineless boneless in the face
of
that light that blasted through space and cut into the
atmosphere
right above my head to form a new rainbow of colors on a new
day
of decisions and heartaches and elation and waves of laughter
and tears
it all washes down a microwave breakfast that grows my
cancerous
disconnect into a malignancy that I pray you could pull from
my gullet
and wrench from my soul in one last ditch attempt to love me a
little more

before the electronic warning on all the devices go off all at once inside
the vacant place you once stood and smiled like you would never leave
before I did...
Let Stand 1-2 Minutes and Enjoy.
Caution: Product Will Be HOT!

Dreams Of Larkspur Landing

through the stone cut slit windows
a fortress of beaten souls guarded
closely by forgotten ghosts
target practice echoing across
concrete floors of unread poetics
come on like syntax of the night
dancing inside eyelids that picture
moonlight on the bay   dancing moonlight
like you know her name   again and again
the steel hitting you with its stillness
rapid fire cold embrace from all sides
remember silk roads less traveled see lights
know the schedule of the ferry by heart   alone
night's eye of imagined disembarkation   last
                           crowd
                           exits
onto ramp out to parked cars driven away
to sausalito, to tiburon, to san rafael, to corte madera
laying there silent on padded steel comeuppance
envisioning welcome home times a hundred
someone caught the last ferry just in time
the crack of distant gunfire   practicing to hit you
                    maybe tomorrow
cannot muffle the distant ferry   foghorn wailing
like mournful dream of a lover crying   tears falling
down into unrequited grave   dark feeling
                  choked back
                 back into reality
cannot crack now like this   tears are weakness
when they stream into awareness   of other souls
warehoused too close for comfort   the parking lot
next to the landing   is full of fog and ghosts
no room for tears here   all good byes already said
not even an echo left   no escape   silver light moments
  pin point   pin prick   pin point   droplet

all that flashes is not precious enough to remember
not painful enough to forget   in the lost hurt of it
one day   maybe   a ride to there   from here to   away, far
away

Fighting For It Seems Pointless Sometimes

it was never really
safe in this time zone
or in this area code
or this state of
confusion

it was always imperative
to be on point
to be on guard
to be under
the gun

if it was done right
it would be the
gift of invisibility
with silence
in a crowd
of loud
noises

people can be beat to death
trial and error has proven
this point to me
but my fingers
get smashed
get broken
in the process

bigger men are better
to beat on
smaller men tend to
carry weapons that
they use with a tenacity
the process of going from
thinking this would be easy
to fighting for your life can

become very painful
can become very messy

my stepfather told me once
when I was young and angry
"you can kill people the way
you lose you temper, make
sure you don't kill anyone
over something that
is bullshit"

men who raised me to
fight also raised me to
kill, but never told me
to do it
never wanted to talk
about it out loud
wanted me to be
quiet and efficient
rather than
loud and obvious
always making it clear
I would wear my decisions
like a second skin
for all time
being known
more for the
decisions
than who I
would really be

I have never wanted to fight
with women
but we have fought
anyways
fair or not
it never really
seemed to matter

I was gonna lose the fight
no matter what

the scars and the wounds
that never heal
are never easy
to see with a
naked eye

the blood that is lost
renews itself
the skin that is lost
grows back
the sleep that is lost
becomes a
waking
damnation
that quickly becomes
a path away from
freedom
in a world that
becomes dark
too early

lights out
can mean so
many things that
cause the heart to
skip a beat in the middle
of a moment where you thought
you might make it without anyone
ever noticing that you were crying
inside
while laughing on the outside
after no joke was told
that you could hear
over the noise
of the crowd

Death Is A Soft Vision, Always Beckoning

she stares so cold into now
taking away every last breath
she holds hands with us all
soon enough
she ends lifetimes
with a lick of lips
with a slight smile
without any noticeable
change of expression
or exasperating sound
coming from her throat
not because she
does not care
more so, because
she has held the hands of those
that even she felt deserved
another chance
but, it was not to be
so she goes about her business
a long, infinite stare in her eyes
that has lasted forever
it is a forever that is
so long so that
no one knows
more than her
that
most likely
it will last
forever more
never stopping
for anyone, least of all
for her

Oshima Island

there is a beach under the pressure
of overwhelming lifelessness
humanity spawned frail
like unfortunate jellyfish
like too much happened
this world is like that
pressure coming down
nuclear poison seeping out
hearts broken in grief and loss
some drifting away like cherry blossoms
blown askance by errant breeze like it was
almost spring on the shore where the land
and the sea took out the time for a world
that was built on the edges so fragile as
this while all that was known to some
was lost in heaps of debris   lost in
the smallest tears of a child   in the
shouts of emotion left out in the open
on the beach under pressure   on the island
under pressure   on the minds of the world
under pressure   this is our modern time
of relinquished sorrows   for those that fall
against the interchanging narratives of loss
weeping out their broken hearts burst with
pain overflowing as we see a world that is
so temporary where we saw it as permanent
so lasting is the stampede of shocking sorrows
this shall be a springtime with a faint whimper
of grateful joy for life as it all dangles on this precipice
as we all dangle on this precipice above this beach together
searching for survivors and pieces of lost lives for memorial

Hayes And Diviz
for K-Dub, a.k.a Kwanz, a.k.a Rick Fairley, Jr.

he always said to never cry for him
to the youngsters on the block
they thought he was crazy
he came from all over
moved all about
knew all
things
he always spoke of the danger in the heart
to the youngsters on the block back then
they would listen to his theories based
on much experience in the actions
of hearts turned cold and dark
they were amazed that he
still lived to be there
to tell them about
the danger that
they knew was
out there
waiting
he always spoke of love that escaped his reach
to the youngsters on the block as they listened
to the explanation of how fingertips can't
reach money and love at the same time
the sign of poverty is to reach for money
hoping love will come sooth you later when
you are a rich man but what happens is you
can't stand waiting for love so you spend all of
the money trying to get love to hurry up quickly
but by the time it is attracted back again you are
much too broke to keep it close so its back to reaching
for love for money for love for money for money for money
where is love in all of that, youngster?
it is in the curling swirls of swisher sweet smoke
rising up above cognac with cork plugs in the neck

because that is all the love you need in moments that
you are just waiting for love to make it back
love will make it back if you are determined
love will make it back if you are committed
love will make it back eventually for you
you have to just believe in one love
for everything that comes back
for you, for anybody, for everybody
it is coming back for me
sooner than you, youngster
he put the gun in the hand
of the youngster
pointed him in a direction
gave him an idea
the youngster had heart
was not dreadful
of the outcome
did his best
to make it out
to make it back
he always told the youngster you have to make it
on your own by your own hand upon the wheel
the youngster listened close and quiet
he made his own way with his hand
heavy on the wheel always
he listened close
but the OG was wrong about one thing
it came back for the youngster
before it came back for the OG
so the OG lets a tear go for the youngster
because life ain't never been fair anyway
he is just sitting back waiting for something
to make it back soon
while it just seems like it keeps going away
its gotta come for him too still
one muthafuckin day

Parole Office

in a room too small
in a moment too heavy
the question is posed
as if there was a choice
"you don't mind, do you?"

the pencils are always sharp here
everything has its own report to be in
lives are filed in the folders for safety
years are folded into lives for safety
file the safety into folders by the year
every duplicate in triplicate until
there is a number for every
human just like in the bible

time clicks here with its own echo chamber
waiting, always waiting, for your number
everyone is coughing and uncomfortable
all eyes look tearful and red
this is the end of the road
that hides a new beginning
it never looks that way
in the dreams that
dance above cons
as they lay their
heads on the
plastic pillows
huddled under
bob barker's
makeshift
blankets
shivering
out silent
prayers
on steel bunks
broken people

in a people
warehouse
waiting for
a number
to be
called

this is not a dream machine
dreams never take this long
reality is what you get here
it is punitive for crimes
both committed and perceived
it is the arbiter of the pain
between victims and perps
these officers in an office
here is what you get
month in, month out
year after year
until you are done
with the room
or until
the room
is done
with you

your life is only as good
as the last fiery hoop
that you jumped
through
successfully

Pretty

she sends pictures from her phone
to show what it looks like there with her

waking up in warmth and softness
with her naked embrace all around

she sends words of encouragement
to those who stumble along, alone

she wants to give hopeful moments away
like they are an innocent dreams shared

maybe she is like a light lick of love
right behind the ear, soft breath on the
moist skin right after
a kind word, in a hushed tone of sexy

there are harder edges than the playful ones
that she pushes all thoughts toward
but, she does not care about them now

she means well, but may be too young to know
she seems to want to share so much, so freely

she may not mean well at all, but she may be
too damaged to care

(maybe she doesn't realize, I have seen it all before)

she might be all that is needed or wanted
in pictures sent from phones
too pretty to hold close right now
too distant to stir much more
than a smile

but, still
I can't help but think
in another place and time
that I might love her, too

Conversion

it becomes something else
not completely unexpectedly
but a mystery, nonetheless
expectations crumble to dust
and new forms of past lives
take shape and grow into
self-sufficient dreams become
bankrupt nightmares
a person goes from an
upright position with a
head held high that
took years of struggle
to achieve just for a
fleeting moment
of false pride
and now they collapse
into a ball of broken humanity
huddling on the ground in a
fetal position
waiting to go out
the same way they came in
only the end isn't near as
the last measurement foretold
and this moment expands
like a growing vacuum
that pulls past and future
into the present
collapsing into an
unforseen direction
that has become the only
space to move into and begin
a slow and tedious crawl forward
into a kneeling position that would be
a foundation for a new beginning
a new life
a last sparkle

of a dying ember
as it catches an autumn
breeze and soars into the
diminishing
twilight sky

Last Words Of My Skid Row Queen

I have been looking for you
not knowing what I was
looking for
I have been looking for you
not knowing what I was
going to find
I have been searching out
your form in the wilderness
of concrete jungle streets
I have been seeking that
comfort that comes from
finding what I need
finding what I want
amidst the random
flotsam and jetsam
of the chaotic life
here on the asphalt
here on the sidewalk
caked with dirty resolutions
that have been
cast aside like
unanswered prayers
left to be picked through
in last chance dumpsters
there are many
unnoticed flowers
dying from neglect
blooming with promises
of an endless after life
that must be better
that the before
of this one
I have been looking for you
losing track of time
losing my mind

lost in this world
not quite into
the next world
living off of the scraps
of your forgotten life
of your empty promise
of your lost hunger
for my love

Lay Low

never bring with you anything
that was not useful in escape

never leave behind anything
that would draw you out
into the vulnerable open
of space and time

never speak of names
never let anyone speak
of your own
never be identified
never be seen

never spend more than
a few moments
seconds
being sentimental

never again
be naive
eyes
wide open

squint now
as if acid
is in your eyes
placed there
by the
treachery
of fools

move to a darker place
run silently
through the night

move slowly
through the day

never look back

never

By The Streetlights Of Sausalito Reflected In The Bay

sitting in the driver's seat motionless on Bridgeway
looking out on black water rippling toward shadowed sea walls
alone
waiting for an end to emptiness like this but only echoes return
what is the point of waiting for anything?
what is the point of pointlessness ?
this is not time spent very well
this is not time well spent at all
this is not time to spend here anymore
the price of its passing is too high
these streets lead to a dark water solitude
these are the moments way past spent
they are as empty as the water is of breathable air
they are as empty as the shadows are of light
they are as barren as these late night
streets of Sausalito
are of lovers
or even ghosts of lovers
that at least haunt love
with remnants to touch
with memories to feel
this is just a profound nothingness
absent like a truant student never to return
incoherent in a perpetual delinquency
it is just the wind between wharf and water
it is just me between darkness and shadows
away from literally lit up streetlights that shine in the distance
without the ability to outdistance the stars
that shine down from the humble greatness
of vast distances high above this intertwined loneliness

invisible silica gel contrails smeared across the night sky
refract staircase
bursts of light beams off of stars that radiate like needles of
shattered

prisms that sparkle the incandescent color spectrum of lost and
found
love in an empty box universe

sitting in lonely jazz solitudes
parked car solution
make it go away
the sensation of time and distance
the sensation of it all slipping away
the way it slips out and around the corner
this is how the aftermath corrects itself
in a timely manner
by reflection of subtraction
by visions of refraction
then nothing left to do
but move on down the road
before another sunrise
catches the real truth of it

Delicacy

freedom, more or less
is on a constant rise upward
over a long time line

you wouldn't know it from
where you are at now
but, it is a historical
fact

unless we lose sight of it all
in a hopeless moment
of want and need
where we refuse
all love

we deny our refusal as fact
we embrace insanity
in the form of false truth
about ourselves
about our lives

our thoughts wander in denial

(we think we have love)
keeping it close
in a heart shaped box
edged with lace
filled with candies
sweet delicacies

all of this is a gift
all of this giving
is necessary

hands touch softly

what hands once rendered
away into a harsh hold
that choked life
tore down freedom
like crabs in a bucket
can't let go
of each others legs

Only If You Got Em'

I get off the phone with my mom
on the other end, not a lot to say
the hiemer's takes care of it
the awkwardness is long gone
with all the time and memories
as I can see my past vanish
in all the secrets
she will take to the grave
long before the grave takes her
I remember she said once, out loud
maybe not directly to me, but
where I could hear, I was very young
but, I still got it and never forgot it, either
"you can always tell when a woman is a whore
or has ever been one" she said,"by the fact that
she smokes in bed"
I understood somewhat
what she was implying
as I grew older
I knew what she meant
completely
I can not recall clearly
if there were ashtrays on the nightstand in her bedroom
way back then
but, in nights full of terrorized sleep I find them
there in the darkness
just before the violence of many episodes plays out
in an avalanche of sinew and mayhem covered in blood
full of the sounds of screams and pleas for a mercy
that never comes in time
I wake up with a jolt to notice the phone ringer going
so I answer it and it is a friend, not really a friend
my old cell mate from a lock up
we used to whisper about ways to escape
late at night when the summertime heat made sleep impossible

we were young and clever back then
even in our beaten state of incarceration
but now he coughs and talks in graveled tones
he tells me, straightforward, "the hep and TB is gaining",
I shiver at my luck with both, hoping it is more real
than his dying voice, "and this bitch keeps smoking in bed,
as if she is trying to kill me quicker"
I tell him, "she is just blind to your suffering because she
loves you so much it hurts to face the truth about your
condition"
there is a wheezing pause in the conversation at this point
"I am too close to death to hear that bullshit from you"
he growls in a hacking restraint, "she is a whore, and you know
it"
he retorts through what must have been gritted dentures
I hang up, because I haven't had a drink in years, I don't want
one now
but, I am feeling a little better
maybe just because
I was able to learn something about life
early on
that stuck with me
long enough to mean something
even if it only meant that I was wrong
about how I should address the dying
and how lucky I am that
my girl doesn't smoke in bed
or even in the house
for that matter

Far Away Grand Daughter

washed out runs of desert chaparral dripping like liquid
candelabra
songs sung low and sweetly to sleeping babies dreaming
storms pass through their minds as they reach a new home
thunder rolls across the dunes toward the mountains
as they stand so superstitious in the distance
minds eye is upon the rose bud as it blooms
a winter wonderment in this flooded land above the delta
with currents lulled into tranquil riffs against the rocks and
cacti
sleep now baby girl and dream of songs on windy nights
like lonely horns of sounding love come for you in waves

water levels are higher than the highest ground below the
waiting station
the noise of rushing movements is like a lullaby that keeps her
silent
a tempest takes no pleasure in its work tonight, but it is
unrelenting
as sands of shifting clockworks on ancient rhythms shift away
from us
pouring all that is historical into the waiting gulf's depression
feeding its desire for lost artifact of sun bleached soul inside
bone
afterward a treasure of relics born anew to coming solar storms
marking new calendars with story become legend become fact
taught in minds that age and decay as these babies sleep
through
this tumultuous monsoon that brings a sacred heart to her
dreams
as she sleeps peaceful under blankets of new tradition woven
with old love
these blooms of yellow rose so unnatural in their scarce beauty
wishing on their bright colors that beam against the red stones
gives dreams of safe passage to growing limbs of love

that reach up past stars and moon toward a new sunrise
like a ship to rescue unwary travelers that go back and forth
in the coldest night of stricken arid plains illuminated blue
then phosphorescent under lightning bursts that belie fingers
pushed down into the earth by their electric arthritic extension
digging up graves of lost flowers that never bloom in sunlight
only are they now revealed in visual echos of bolted aftermath
she stirs as if to listen to the songs of coyote chasing itself
away
into swirling winds of wailing sorrow that she has yet to know
in its place the love of movement to hold the hands that give
strength
making flowering petals pull out of stems grasping to
outstretched arms
as if to hug an old man who searches for her across arroyo into
night
just to tell her of the loving pride he has for her before he
closes
his tired eyes to dream of a desert floor covered in blooming
flowers
each one a rare magnificence that points upward to a new sun

the sun rises into dawn after the storm relents into passing
she opens her eyes as if to say hello for the first time

Literary Green Mood

maybe I should read more books
so I wont be so jealous of the ones
you are reading right now

maybe I should write more books
so I wont be so jealous of the ones
you are writing right now

maybe I should
maybe I should

I know I could
be singing and dancing
without a care for
anything else at all
right now

maybe
      I should

maybe
      I shall
           maybe

Xmas Eve Plans on San Pablo & Grand

nutrition in small amounts
mostly garbage calories
feeling the empty
feeling the pit
opening wide
a line forms
around the block
portioned out
for all the fallen
spirits of the day
all feet tired, belly hungry
(looking toward
xmas eve in west oakland)
rough & calloused hands
reach out for
a paper plate
w/ potato salad
past the due date
hot dog on a
stale slice of bread
pint o' milk
on the verge of
expiration
this is a catholic
charity
stretched to its limit
on it's own idea
of a sacred eve
that is more
like a scary
superstition
for this battered flock
of unforgiven
forsaken souls
as they stroll away

leaving bags full
of soiled disposable
utensils &
maybe enough on the belly
to get a good hustle underway
so later that night
after a long pull
on a plastic bottle
of fake vodka
& a hit on blackened glass tube
that once held a paper &
wire rose
sputtering lighter
igniting a piece of
a burnt up
brillo
into smoke
shaky hands
passing it on
the half empty gut
churning on the last of
the giveaway meal
from a forgotten
moment
earlier
in the day
made up of
mostly
lips &
assholes

Clean It Up Nicely

you clean up all the mess
you repair all the damage
you paint over all of the
old & worn out
you replace broken glass
you straighten up what
has become crooked
you plant flowers
in the garden
veggies that you can eat
sit down on the front step
after it is all put back into
some kind of new order
but, then
you have to know
that whatever you are
wearing
shoes & clothes & such
is as dirty as the disaster
that you just made go away
so you might as well
strip down to bare skin
run naked through the spray
of the turned up garden hose
& leave those clothes & things
down by the curb for someone
less fortunate than you
before you go back inside
your new home
just so
you really start over
brand new & fresh
& never look back
to that curb
or to that gutter

that lies just beyond it
never wonder who
is wearing those
old clothes & things
it is none of your
business anymore

For The Ones

seascapes haunted forever never seem so cold
not as cold as lifeless skin is to my touch

ghosts are not real, just a gathering of memories
twirling around my world like a maniacal jetstream

some get buried, some get burned, some get so lost
they are never found wandering back to wave good bye
one last time

I keep a caring list of sensations memorized inside my heart
in a rainproof locker of cherished love that I had to let go of
to keep it moving
>   *you can never look back*
>   *it only reveals lightposts*
>   *that lead to the desert*

motel room key I left behind with her body
bullet fragment I pulled from his wound
blood soup pushed through her wrist red gills
hospital sounds at night while rounds are made
around her body as it succumbs while interns
trade box scores on the latest games with levity
I laugh too, especially when others speak of selfish anger
as if their jealousy wasn't obvious concerning who takes
certain dark initiatives that wrench hearts from chests
nothing really poetic here, just memories of loss
gathered like acorns in the fall to be glued to thankful
paper cut outs of a child's hand that made a lost ashtray as well
people are all like loaded guns in my life, waiting to fire
until the chamber is empty, a god in the sky never reloads them
I have watched friends wait forever, staring at flags, stone,
bullet holes
in the stucco ceiling, leather jackets, bus tokens, burnt spoons,

grassy hills, subway cars, crashing waves, freeway off ramps
as if they were keys to some unseen lock that would turn and
click
reality would open anew and we would all get one more chance
past the stop of last chances, but it never happens
sadly, but honestly, more honest than any truth you will ever
know
it never happens

I remember, afterward, how
she carried a piece of his skull
in a locket around her neck
her neck became thinner
as days went by
I never saw her again
after the last night I saw her
tenderloin corner, thin as smoke
waiting for her last ghost that
was never coming
until she took the last gasp, instead

Dealing With It

all these cities built on hilltops
above crushing sounds of waves
driven ashore by divine currents
welling up from below the center
of the altruistic plane of reality

they seethe with fog banks
they broil with windy surf
they writhe with traffic and
pedestrian hopes of future
relative to dream states that
have little kernels of love
hidden deep inside themselves

fear comes smashing against it all
in storm fronts that bear down on top
of the highest aspirations against darkness
pushing down everything against the pounding
of the ocean at the shoreline
sinking partial aspects of
hope like drowned victims
submerged in receding
floodwaters of eternal
damnation

this road snakes the coastline
connecting these cities with ribbons
of asphalt resurrections at each
crosswalk intersection

these roads once ran like arteries
of smuggled bits of hopeful dreams
hidden away inside the math of the deal
hidden away in the conversion of weights
hidden away in the increments of measures

hidden away in the trunks and baggage of drama
they had to get through at any cost
every mile marker was a conviction
in an attempt at living while the
concealed truth was always death
death by the code
death by the false pride
death by the hand that held yours last
death by the heart that failed and betrayed
death by the smoke of the barrel or the edge of the blade
death by the last knotted truth around your bruised neck
death by the executioner in his official appointment
no pardon from any government leader who had
hoped more for re-election than love would allow
the gallows were built in the mind long ago
we lived forever in the flats below the cities
they tower above while we hid most of our lives
behind closed doors with alarming intentions
terror knew no boundaries until boredom
became the only freedom from the tension
all remaining teeth here were ground to mortar
to build the last bridge along the falling cliffs
so the people could never know what wonder
has been smuggled around them in the noble
beauty of pines underneath skies of blue
with intermittent fog banks to camouflage
the delivery of ill gotten goods to
the dark market below cities
built upon hills above the
oceans ever changing
shoreline of faith

911

eclipsing 47 years
looking down the barrel at 48
beginning to wonder what 50
is gonna look like
as it begins to look back
in the lonely mirror
up until now
after all this time
I had never made the call
I had never dialed 911
until I had to at work
drunks were out of
control
I hesitated
years of being steel
against that call
avowed to never make it
in a moment
I hesitate
it is bothersome
I make the call
talk to the operator
my co-workers
the bar manager
the general manager
looking at me
like I am crazy
they are right
it is driving me nuts
I think about it all the way home
I crossed a line
broke my code of
self preservation
the call emanated from my phone
I am on a computer log

my voice recorded with
a record of my phone number
that is on an account
with my real name on it
my life has changed
dramatically
I try not to hyperventilate
on the drive home
then later on
the 911 operator
calls me back
as I get ready for bed
I tell her it is all taken care of
we will file a report tomorrow
I hang up and turn out the lights
haunted by fear
I know
for certain
it will never be the same again
my life has changed
in a way that I never saw coming
it makes me nervous
just like being
on Facebook
this shit is permanent
it will never be the same
ever again

Gone With/Gone Without

we are soaking in it

it is in the silent graves
buried alive last night
never again found
in the light of days
lost without sun

it is in the open fields
incurred by progress
overgrown with
new concrete
metaphors

it is in the gunpowder keg
ready to ignite into a bad
calamity for someone
else at our expense

it is in the misty rains
along the coast roads
cooling the engines
that have run too wild
for much too long

the piss is in the wind
the piss is in the sea
the piss is left on
desert playas
drying into clods
of salty
clumps

we drink it like whiskey
we smoke it like glass

we shoot it like dope
we lick it like acid
we lap it up like milk
we suck it up like cum
but it is still our piss

we are made of the same piss
it is in the jelly of our eyes
no matter the colorings
no matter the genes
no matter the make-up

the piss slides through us all
imperative at urethreal release
pushing against all bladders
of time & space
burning like gasoline
in cocktails of
fiery explosions
becoming
bursts of light
blinding
the gelatin visuals
of humanoid desires
crouched in caves
skittering across plains
in search of sustenance
in search of prey
in search of sex
in search of love
fooled by our own
piss stained sheets
that seconds & minutes
take away from hours and days
to make ejaculate pronouncements
that piss all over our pages
that piss off our fellows

that piss & piss
always pissing
it all away
running down
our collective legs
to encircle our tattered feet
puddling out all over ourselves
now thirstily
we drink in more life
just to piss it all out again

War Story

it comes to this sometimes
the oatmeal of days run by
big spoonful after spoonful
sitting uncomfortable with
long moments that talk loud
comparing bullet holes and
blade scars to broken hearts
and warped minds set loose
in a blender of emotions that
chop and mince as wanting is
what guides the shredded up
spirit as it sits bandaged in its
formidable former ingloriousness
telling stories of wars past as
the wars on the horizon
have yet to formulate
a new exit strategy
out of the grand entrance
of leftover dust and ash
waiting on the moment
like clouds gathering
out on the pacific
only that
this depression
is never
tropical

Gravity Change

last lemons fall thudding to the ground
splitting open with powdery mold
during the harvest moon transition
bougainvillea petals burst into magenta confetti
that gathers around in drifts of pinked mulch
thorns point outward from branches exposed
skeletal shapes form from trees that slim
into the reaching forms of bare bark arms
pumpkin spiders bloat into festive orange
hanging on to blustery webs their work
is never done as the air is cooler
the night is longer and longer
the freeze dry air is approaching
everything is falling by morning
down comes the leafiness of the world
wind blown shadiness is weaker now
light drops into these opening spaces
with skyward fingers barely hidden
in the last gloves of foliage

In the Company of Shakespeare
for George Whitman

stuck and broke down
inside the city of lights
waiting on some hustle
slow in coming to me
down the road from
Amsterdam
I don't feel much
like a writer
but after 2 nights
sleeping in the humble
accommodations
of these hallowed
halls of books
& liberation
I keep quiet
I keep the front up
no one can see into
a smuggler's eyes
when they glance
into mine
& when then hustle comes back
just in the nick of time
it suddenly seems too soon
& I leave there
saying farewell to the books
saying farewell to the ghosts
feeling more like a writer
than I ever had before

Birthday Sunrise on a Xmas Morning

the sunbeams come down from over the hill
they say they have been here the whole time
for every circle that was made around them
they say,
they never circled back once
they always stayed in the middle
in between what comes after life
in between what comes before death
there is a sunbeam out there
that never forgets a name
that shines down on you
all throughout your in between days
bouncing at you off the moon at night
coming into your heart when the moment
is just right,
        when the timing is there
       without fail, a sunbeam
       that you can have faith in
        a faith you will never lose
       the sun is always shining
      somewhere, somehow
      it never forgets names
       but, birthdays are forever
       the sun made a promise
        you can go around & around
        never stop circling
        be living or dead
         & the sun keeps its promise
        always
            it will never circle back
            it will always be there
            being the sun
             sending out a sunbeam
             just for you
            that lights the in between
            of everything

a slight oncoming rain at night

these winds breathe across the bay toward the point
howling mad at the anemic capacity of the storm
spilling out nothing but tears of babes falling
like alloy drops loosed from leaden clouds
falling the way golden parachutes might
falling like lead-winged butterflies
to the ground all tempest will eventually fall
to the ground all, to the ground where it will begin anew
waiting under the cover of the darkness & the improbability of
fortune

Ash Wednesday

you can see what is saved
through the peril
of sacrifice

you can see what will live
in the aftermath
of disaster

you can replant fields
you can rebuild shelter
you can impregnate
desire with a newborn
coming of life birthed
into the world come
after the disaster
after the apocalypse
after your god
begins to fall
away from you
just ever so slightly

the city gates have been buried
four stories deep in the ground
for so long as the sun altered
its course
in a vain attempt to regain its vision
when it lost sight of the moon

the children hold hands in a circle
breathing fire as they chant a simple song
embers falling down all around them
they speak an ancient tongue
that has split into two
until
they speak no more

the silence of the world is spawning
before an angry cry will grow to a roar
war is always on the heels of redemption
as the redeemer becomes more well armed
than ever
before

victim of circumstance

a scuffling sound of uncertain footsteps approaches
along a cracked up concrete sidewalk toward a corner
that sits under streetlight illumination in the distance
it precedes the staggering form as it lumbers into
the intersection that blurs into the foreground
with horns headlights panhandlers hookers
& the air essence of lost hope held behind
a shield of false conviction & poverty bravado

the sway of the form that makes the movement stop
nearly sends the immediate world cantilevering into the street
head over heels into the night time intersection of mayhem
the senses uncloud enough to deliver a clear message
"this might not be the lifetime I had wanted"
the night is all icepicks & daggers into a somersault heart
that was left to die in a minefield of uninformed decisions
left laying around like lazy trip wires waiting for victims

the form takes reassurance in the fact that it never knew better
that it never wondered enough out loud in a place where it
could be
properly corrected or advised to alter its course in another
direction
the coming disaster was par for the course, considering the
state
of the world around it & the only good omen lately was that
most folks
had been in some form of desperation just as bad or worse than
what
the present form had been dealing with & then some

the lights were confusing & the cravings were too many for the
form
to keep the moment of clarity in perfect vision enhancement

the blurs came back into focus & the whole stink of the street came back
full force into its nostrils like a rolling herd of buffalo turds on stampede
the form stumbled out dizzily into the crosswalk that it could not see
as straight lines any longer, hoping against hope that the next step
would not be the last as instinct told it that there was a liquor store
on the opposing corner & at least two dollars in change that was presently
burning a hole into the misguided form's last pocket of defense

A One & A Two & A Three

I come here late at night
to scribble words down
to pound keys into stone
to watch with teary eyes as
hazy thoughts are walking away
not able to remember
exactly what I came for
I find myself
spoiled by the loss & failure
like an infantile tantrum
given way to milky orgasm
I can feel myself
treated by the insecure wind
like a champion of fools
on a ship run aground
in shark infested waters

I come here late at night
to get it right for once
after so many wrongs
to let my hair down
from its receding place
atop the lonely mountain of me
where there is a winter coming
that is most likely
destined to be my last
because that is the way
destiny works in overtime
with a clock ticking too loud
to hear the horns of oblivion
howling outside in the tempest

I come here late at night
to forget things that are
unforgettable

to remember
how lucky I am
to remember
how to smile at death
just like I was still a child
to try to let it all go
to try to get it all back
one last time
until
I return here again
when
I come here late at night

When San Pablo Ave. Floods

the rain comes down in Ghost Town
washing hardened sidewalks that
trap the foot steps of hardened living

bedbugs running all the single room occupants
into the torment of deluge from open skies
wringing out on their heads like dirty sponges
being twisted by the hands of some careless creator

the rain seems part of the shipyards, part of the docks
as if the hulls of ships were turned upward as the streets
were put at the bottom of the bay below them

nearby in the weather even longshoremen seek refuge
wait for the rain to let up before they off load the cargo
containers come from exotic ports in far away markets
to be distributed from Oakland as people seem to hide in
the dark shadows or scurry around outside with trash bags
held over their heads or the ones who seem to have left
well enough alone just marching, trudging through the
sheets of downpour as if some wailing siren drew them
on into the night of risen rivers run through the gutters
that proclaim this town as temporary tide pool for the bay
as it soaks in the run off of the broken down huddled
structures that run from Ghost Town to the Lower Bottoms
and into the busy port of call that can't seem to fix what
is wrong with the world no matter how many ships are
pulled through under the half built bridge that attempts
to take over for the old broken one before the next big
world series comes to the bay as it sits behind golden gates
in a promontory of tides against cities and towns that still
need what the gold rush never left behind to just let you
lay down your burden and find some dry shelter from the rain

Los Feliz

soft trail along the hillside   a winter park of sunlight
  foot falls under oak   warm faces smile out
   crisp sounds   radiant   beams of hope
     gabrielinos born here not forgotten
      the treasure not lost, just worn
                         down
                     amidst the
considerable influence of foreign tongues gone mad
  a corporal's name mispronounced in trade
  a corporeal life traded away   stars stream at
                   night
     beauty here among peaceful   *moments*
      light, camera, action   award/reward
       the real love peels away   like old lead paint
eyes that glimmer with heart felt desire   hold us
                   together
   far away lands in far away times   where to
                   now?
    keep us here like captured light
        lost into invisible smoke
       at sunrise above
       hilly footpaths
this was always meant to be a gift given away
  this was always meant to be a place to search out
   this vast desert for an oasis
    this vast shoreline for an anchoring bay
    this loneliness for some momentary
                 companion
                 friendship
                 lover
 shade from winter heat or summer cool
  this was the path   this was the arrival
  walk up to the vista   destination
  watch the birds fly   away

to a distant ocean   of
    happiness   among us
        keep   searching   out   there
          keep   searching
             far   and   wide
      slowly lonely along the peaceful walks
      in this tiny communal memorial
       every footstep given unto

searching

Leading With The Wrong Foot

deep breath before ascent into heaven
never really knew the way before
it must be heaven for those
who stop feeling confusion
who stop sensing doom
in the many platitudes
laid out so carefully
before them now

short exhale before descent into hell
just enough to keep the fire at bay
this was exactly what was expected
it is hell for those of us who never
got it right to begin with or
got a break we had hoped for
this is all just another racket
designed to peel us away from some eternity
that will never look the same as it did in the brochure

Deficit

it feels like the world is about to burst open in protest
but, in reality, most folks are safe at home
unaware that the 7 billionth soul is near
so near it makes it hard to remember
how it was not so long ago
that we were surprised
with the 6 billionth
soul out of
nowhere

it feels like love just walked out the door
to go drunk driving without me
no revolution for her
it is too boring
& mocking me got old
quick,
       so now it's
better to come back to me
later on, in the early morning
all
whiskey stench & cock breath
talking about love with a hidden
anger over unborn children that will
never let go
never be content
with any surrender
like an immortal assassin
it is choking love out from behind
buckling it at it's knees
as I watch helplessly
wondering when
it might be too much
even for me to handle
alone

& in these moments
alone
it feels like it is all over
& maybe it is, maybe it isn't
maybe it is all just a bad joke
or just a worse perception
of what it is
to begin with

from this perspective
it feels pretty bad
& right now
it mostly feels like this:
it feels
like our side is losing
even without ever
winning

so how would we know
the difference
give or take
a billion?
& why is it boring
all of a sudden
to care about it?

Bus Stop Gifts

getting off the bus in west oakland
this afternoon
walking thru the madness all around
boarded up dreams next to
broken down lives
thrown away things
left to disintegrate into
constant reminders
of the fallen out of place
the insanity of falling behind
the dirty truth about care
or the lack thereof
I stumble for a moment
on what must be
a little bit of hope
right where I needed most
right where someone must have left it
just for someone like me
who wants to do what I came to do
with all the love in my heart
I have learned to carry
with me
from those of you
that leave the hope
laying where it is needed most
I pledge this to you
I hope to have some
hope leftover
to leave here
for the next person
as well

The Indelible I

I fell in love
way over my head
way out of my league
far from any homeland
that wandered away from me

I took a stand
alone in the wild
alone in the crowd
wanting my freedom
always beginning with alone
always ending with alone

I felt the loss
it is a feeling that never has really left me
it is a feeling that I go through
the same way you do
I am going through it now
just like all of you are

I saw a slight glimpse
in a dreamlike moment
that looked like this:

I could be a part of you
if you let me
you are all a part of me
because I have let you
I saw us all together
for once
I saw all of us
together
then
I saw nothing

I am waiting on the rest
just like
       you are

Gold

kisses that taste like
warm apple pie
your skin so soft and radiant
as we lie naked in close embrace
on a summer beach just before sunset

the warm wind licks at us
as we lick at each other

your face so bright with
happiness it outshines the
descending sun

your voice drips into my ear
like raw honey that has sat out
on a hot august day
and runs warm and smooth
and sweet

I close my eyes and smile
for a moment
and when I open them again
the last bit of sunlight
is just a glimmer on the waves
and the sky has darkened
with the purple bruising
of dusk oncoming

but, you still radiate that glow
like never before
like a golden memory
that warms
a winter heart
in a prison of
lost dreams

Caught In The Place You Were Last Seen

hot knife wounds sear into flesh
burning its way out from
the hashy insides of
coughed up lungs
standing too long
over lit up stoves
that will cook no
nourishment
they manufacture
only medicine
for ruptured
spirits that
are bleeding
to death
slowly

look at the hands to see who won the fights
it is there in the knuckles bulging out
forever like the fingers drawn into
pathways of eternal crookedness
look at the forearms to see the
scar tissue from defensive wounds
that tell the stories of attempts
at assassination that have failed
to kill the heart but rip the mind
apart in waking nightmares that
have no beginning or end in the
days and nights that come for us
like a parade of warning shots
fired from unseen guard towers
shake it off shake it off shake it off
let the fists unball into hands
let the eyes loosen into an open gaze
let the chest become unconstricted

let the teeth ease into a comfortable place
where they do not crush into each other
tops into bottoms squeezing blood
out of the gums into the saliva around
the tongue that is ravaged from the stress
of the built up anger that covers the pushed down
fear that keeps trying to come up when you
least expect it least expect it least expect it
you must expect it in every moment of
every day from now until some great event
occurs that may set you free as you search for it
over stove tops, in hotel rooms, in motel parking lots
in back alley solitude, in jungle secrecy, in forest tranquility
in the deserts you have wandered alone, in the rivers that run
down canyons in turmoil, inside the shipwrecks on the shores
inside supermarkets, inside cars headed for promising horizons
inside darkened warehouses, inside trucks headed for doom
ahead
in the blackness of space, in the headphones of dj's, in the eyes
of
the willing, in the screams of the damned, in the portion you
are given
in the portion you have taken, inside the heart of your lover,
into the idea
that there is a god that might love you, into the music that plays
only in your mind
into the oceans that surround you, into the oceans inside of
you, inside the ocean

hot spoons leave burnt marks on motel bibles as tributes to true
loneliness
rocked up cocaine cracks us all into pieces of sweaty terror
without screams
hypodermic emotions pierce into fleshy desires that they may
know peace

through the force of insanity and tribulation at the edge of
death's door   as we search
through it all for last hope like hope was a collapsed vein
pill upon pills upon pills upon pills upon pills upon pills
still there is no answer from the void that did not originate
from inside our own mind first then second in the form
of a beckoning light like that of a bush that burns
while talking about the options you have at a life
that seems to have blindsided you into this
chasm of repetition of repetition of repetition
repeating itself over and over and over
again and again and again and again
until you make marks everywhere you go
trying to find a way to predict the next turn
trying to make a turn that is unpredictable
trying to break this manic cycle
trying to stop this crazy thing
trying to get off before
it is too late
it is too late
never never never
just stop for moment
before it catches up again
be free for a moment before
you are never really free again

Broken Hearted

minimal ticking
of little parts

we spoke of
separation
with words
that cut
deep

maximum swelling
of bigger pieces

alone
it was
noticeable
we needed
something more

still
the nerves
can't let go
of the sensation
that the cut was made
too soon for
our own
good

never again
has been
a long
time

never
always is

sight unseen

the sign for
need
is a finger
shaped
like
a hook
the place for
a heart
is a hole
in your
head
the time on
clocks
is a terror
for modern
people
living
in a
modern
world
blinded
by faith
in a mechanical
hope
lost
to them
in front
of their
faces
in a type
of weather
no one
can
predict

Not A Proper Sensei

I am not ready to be the teacher
I would give handguns to kids
the same way they were given to me
tell them firmly
"don't ever let anyone fuck with you, ever."
point them down the canyon
fill their mouth with tequila
every time they hit an empty bottle
that shattered into jagged little pieces
of childhood accomplishment
slap them in the back when they choke on
the bitter taste, fighting for the real air
that is gone & will never return
as I laugh at them struggling
as the desert hawks
circle higher in the sky
than the rancid turkey vultures
higher & maybe too close
to the midday rays of sunlight
that evaporate the tears of young children
that were never really taught how to behave
that were never really taught the difference
between love & behavior
the things they were taught
they were taught so as to prepare them to
just how to win at all costs, no matter what
just how to keep fear & signs of collapse hidden
just how to love the smell of burning cordite
& gasoline against heavy metal & blued steel
just how to pretend that tequila tasted like love
& to never let a burning throat be confused
with a burning soul on fire
I could never teach anyone that
I will never want to pass that on

Here Comes A Grandchild

you come loping into this world full force
nearly full grown with purpose before you are born
as the tides do their thing   as the rivers run to delta
as the pheasant multiply in waiting   as the laughter
                                        increases
   you are forming hand signals in my dreams
asking me questions I am compelled to answer
   looking up at stars and knowing what they will mean
but, for now
                just being an infant in waiting as long as the
sundial is in the shadows of every second we wait
                we wait to see you writhing in new birth
                we wait to deliver our unburdened love
                we wait for mothers to be at ease now
   all will be revealed as the crown is passed on into the light
none will be lost from here in the moment it takes to bless us
all
this is the part of existence that is much more than mere
survival
this is where the fractured walls of love get repaired a little
more
with each new born breath taken
with each sigh and sound overheard
with every hug and kiss that is meant to nurture and welcome
into this world   into this world   into this world   now
            you   are   born

to be new again

things fall in & out
of place
as worlds turn toward
darkness & daylight
in intervals
coated
by life
& lubricated
by experience
as the spasms roll
across the linear landscape
nearly seven billion moments
that feel different right now
each one about to spark
a chain reaction in an
unforeseen direction
that will cross the lines
& connect the dots of
scattered atoms across
a random pattern of hope
& pain & love & fear
like an awkward faith
that there was a breath
taken from some strange
wind across time
as a breath was given back
without resistance
or realization
of self

THE END

A. Razor was born in Brooklyn, N.Y. in 1963, but was brought to California at the age of 1. He was raised with a strong desire to read and write, but an even greater desire to survive his circumstances, which has aided his experience and longevity so far. He began writing and publishing around 1980 in various underground zines and publications, first in the Los Angeles area, then ever expanding outward from there as he was discovered by Drew Blood Press, Ltd. in 1984, where he published 11 chapbooks up to 1995. He has read his work at many readings and spoken word events over the years and been published in many types of publications, ranging from those that are considered reputable to those that are of ill repute. He has fought hard to live and express his art in many different ways and in many different places. He became a member of the Hollywood Institute of Poetics in Los Angeles, CA in 2009. He has participated recently in the Poets In Prison panel at Beyond Baroque and the 2011 ALOUD reading series held at the Downtown Los Angeles Public Library. His writing has always explored the world that he has sought to be a part of and to rebel against at the same paradoxical moment. He has traveled extensively, seeking and enduring everything from homelessness and imprisonment to serenity and peace.

MORE PUNK HOSTAGE PRESS BOOKS

Fractured (2012) by **Danny Baker**

A. Razor
Better Than A Gun In A Knife Fight (2012)
Drawn Blood: Collected Works
From D.B.P.LTD., 1985-1995 (2012)
Beaten Up Beaten Down (2012)
Small Catastrophes In A Big World (2012)
Half- Century Status (2013)
Days Of Xmas Poems (2014)
Puro Purismo (2021)

Iris Berry
The Daughters Of Bastards (2012)
All That Shines Under The Hollywood Sign (2019)

Impress (2012) by **C.V. Auchterlonie**

Tomorrow, Yvonne - Poetry & Prose For Suicidal Egoists (2012) by **Yvonne De la Vega**

Miracles Of The Blog: A Series (2012) by **Carolyn Srygley- Moore**

8th & Agony (2012) by **Rich Ferguson**

Jack Grisham
Untamed (2013)
Code Blue: A Love Story ~ Limited Edition (2014)

Dennis Cruz
Moth Wing Tea (2013)
The Beast Is We (2018)

*Blood Music (*2013) by **Frank Reardon**

Showgirl Confidential (2013) by **Pleasant Gehman**

Yeah, Well... (2014) by **Joel Landmine**

History Of Broken Love Things (2014) by **SB Stokes**

MORE PUNK HOSTAGE PRESS BOOKS

Stealing The Midnight From A Handful Of Days
(2014) by **Michele McDannold**

Dreams Gone Mad With Hope (2014) by **S.A. Griffin**

How To Take A Bullet And Other Survival Poems
(2014) by **Hollie Hardy**

Dead Lions (2014) by **A.D. Winans**

Nadia Bruce- Rawlings
Scars (2014)
Driving in The Rain (2020)

*WHEN I WAS A DYNAMITER, Or, how a Nice Catholic Boy Became a
Merry Prankster, a Pornographer, and a Bridegroom Seven Times*
(2014) by **Lee Quarnstrom.**

Alexandra Naughton
I Will Always Be Your Whore/Love Songs For Billy Corgan (2014) *You
Could Never Objectify Me More Than I've Already Objectified Myself*
(2015)

No Parachutes To Carry Me Home (2015) by **Maisha Z Johnson**

#1 Son And Other Stories (2017) by **Michael Marcus**

LOOKING FOR JOHNNY, The Legend of Johnny Thunders
(2018) by **Danny Garcia**

Burden Of Concrete (2020) by **William S. Hayes**

Dillinger's Thompson (2020) by **Todd Moore**

*$100-A-Week Motel (*2021) by **Dan Denton**

www.ingramcontent.com/pod-product-compliance
Lightning Source LLC
LaVergne TN
LVHW041153080426
835511LV00006B/572